Chinese Literature, Ancient and Classical

Chinese Literature, Ancient and Classical

by
André Lévy

translated by
William H. Nienhauser, Jr.

Indiana University Press
Bloomington and Indianapolis

This book is a publication of

Indiana University Press
601 North Morton Street
Bloomington, Indiana 47404-3797 USA

www.indiana.edu/~iupress

Telephone orders 800-842-6796
Fax orders 812-855-7931
Orders by e-mail iuporder@indiana.edu

The paper used in this publication meets the minimum requirements
of American National Standard for Information Sciences—Permanence
of Paper for Printed Library Materials, ANSI Z39.48-1984.

Manufactured in the United States of America

Library of Congress Cataloging-in-Publication Data

Lévy, André, date
    [La littérature chinoise ancienne et classique. English]
    Chinese literature, ancient and classical / by André Lévy ;
translated by William H. Nienhauser, Jr.
        p.   cm.
    Includes index.
    ISBN 0-253-33656-2 (alk. paper)
    1. Chinese literature—History and criticism.   I. Nienhauser,
William H.   II. Title.
PL2266.L48   2000
895.1'09—dc21   99-34024

1   2   3   4   5   05   04   03   02   01   00

For my own early translators of French,
Daniel and Susan

Contents

Translator's Preface

I first became interested in translating André Lévy's history of Chinese literature, *La littérature chinoise ancienne et classique* (Paris: Presses Universitaires de France, 1991), in 1996, after finding it in a bookshop in Paris. I read sections and was intrigued by Professor Lévy's approach, which was modeled on literary genres rather than political eras. I immediately thought about translating parts of the book for my graduate History of Chinese Literature class at the University of Wisconsin, a class in which the importance of dynastic change was also downplayed.

Like many plans, this one was set aside. Last spring, however, when the panel on our field's desiderata headed by David Rolston at the 1998 Association for Asian Studies Meeting pronounced that one of the major needs was for a concise history of Chinese literature in about 125 pages (the exact length of Professor Lévy's original text), I revived my interest in this translation. I proposed the book to John Gallman, Director of Indiana University Press, and John approved it almost immediately–but, not before warning me that this kind of project can take much more time than the translator originally envisions. Although I respect John's experience and knowledge in publishing, I was sure I would prove the exception. After all, what kind of trouble could a little book of 125 pages cause?

I soon found out. Professor Lévy had originally written a much longer manuscript, which was to be published as a supplementary volume to Odile Kaltenmark-Ghéquier's *La Littérature chinoise* (Paris: Presses Universitaires de France, 1948)[1] in the *Que sais-je?* (What Do I Know?) series. This concept, however, was soon abandoned, and it

---

[1] Several decades ago Anne-Marie Geoghegan translated this volume as *Chinese Literature* (New York: Walker, 1964).

was decided to publish the Lévy "appendix" as a separate volume–in 125 pages. Professor Lévy was then asked to cut his manuscript by one-third. As a result, he was sometimes forced to presume in his audience certain knowledge that some readers of this book–for example, undergraduate students or interested parties with little background in Chinese literature–may not have. For this reason, working carefully with Professor Lévy, I have added (or revived) a number of contextual sentences with these readers in mind. More information on many of the authors and works discussed in this history can be found in the entries in *The Indiana Companion to Traditional Chinese Literature* (volumes 1 and 2; Bloomington: Indiana University Press, 1986 and 1998). Detailed references to these entries and other relevant studies can be found in the "Suggested Further Reading" sections at the end of each chapter (where the abbreviated reference *Indiana Companion* refers to these two volumes).

I also discovered that re-translating Professor Lévy's French translations of Chinese texts sometimes resulted in renditions that were too far from the original, even in this age of "distance education." So I have translated almost all of the more than 120 excerpts of original works directly from the original Chinese, using Professor Lévy's French versions as a guide wherever possible.

All this was done with the blessing and cooperation of the author. Indeed, among the many people who helped with this translation, I would like to especially thank Professor André Lévy for his unflinching interest in and support of this translation. Professor Lévy has read much of the English version, including all passages that I knew were problematic (there are no doubt others!), and offered comments in a long series of letters over the past few months. Without his assistance the translation would never have been completed. Here in Madison, a trio of graduate students have helped me with questions about the Chinese texts: Mr. Cao Weiguo 曹衛國, Ms. Huang Shu-yuang 黃叔垣, and Mr. Shang Cheng 尚琤. They saved me from innumerable errors and did their work with interest and high spirits. Mr. Cao also helped by pointing out problems in my interpretation of the original French. Mr. Scott W. Galer of Ricks College read the entire manuscript and offered a number of invaluable comments. My wife, Judith, was unrelenting in her demands on behalf of the general reader. The most careful reader was, however, Jane Lyle of Indiana University Press, who painstakingly copy-edited the text. If there is a literary style to this translation, it is due to her efforts.

My thanks, too, to the Alexander von Humboldt Foundation which supported me in Berlin through the summer of 1997 when I first read Professor Lévy's text, and especially to John Gallman, who stood behind this project from the beginning.

Madison, Wisconsin, 16 February 1999 (Lunar New Year's Day)

Chinese Literature,
Ancient and Classical

Introduction

Could one still write, as Odile Kaltenmark-Ghequier did in 1948 in the *What Do I Know* series Number 296, which preceded this book, that "the study of Chinese literature, long neglected by the Occident, is still in its infancy?"[1] Yes and no. There has been some spectacular progress and some foundering. At any rate, beginning at the start of the twentieth century, it was Westerners who were the first–followed by the Japanese, before the Chinese themselves–to produce histories of Chinese literature. Not that the Chinese tradition had not taken note of an evolution in literary genres, but the prestige of *wen* 文, signifying both "literature" and "civilization," placed it above history–anthologies, compilations, and catalogues were preferred. Moreover, the popular side of literature–fiction, drama, and oral verse–because of its lack of "seriousness" or its "vulgarity," was not judged dignified enough to be considered *wen*.

Our goal is not to add a new work to an already lengthy list of histories of Chinese literature, nor to supplant the excellent summary by Odile Kaltenmark–Ghéquier which had the impossible task of presenting a history of Chinese literature in about a hundred pages. Our desire would be rather to complement the list by presenting the reader with a different approach, one more concrete, less dependent on the dynastic chronology. Rather than a history, it is a picture–inevitably incomplete–of Chinese literature of the past that this little book offers.

Chinese "high" literature is based on a "hard core" of classical training consisting of the memorization of texts, nearly a half-million characters for every candidate who reaches the highest competitive examinations. We might see the classical art of writing as the arranging, in an appropriate and astute fashion, of lines recalled by memory, something

---

[1]Odile Kaltenmark-Ghéquier, "Introduction," *La littérature chinoise* (Paris: Presses Universitaires de France, 1948), p. 5; "Que sais-je," no. 296.

that came almost automatically to traditional Chinese intellectuals.

The goal of these writers was not solely literary. They hoped through their writings to earn a reputation that would help them find support for their efforts to pass the imperial civil-service examinations and thereby eventually win a position at court. Although there were earlier tests leading to political advancement, the system that existed nearly until the end of the imperial period in 1911 was known as the *jinshi* 進士 or "presented scholar" examination (because successful candidates were "presented" to the emperor), and was developed during the late seventh and early eighth centuries A.D. It required the writing of poetry and essays on themes set by the examiners. Successful candidates were then given minor positions in the bureaucracy. Thus the memorization of a huge corpus of earlier literature and the ability to compose on the spot became the major qualifications for political office through most of the period from the eighth until the early twentieth centuries.

These examinations, and literature in general, were composed in a classical, standard language comparable to Latin in the West. This "classical" language persisted by opposing writing to speech through a sort of partial bilingualism. The strict proscription of vulgarisms, of elements of the spoken language, from the examinations has helped to maintain the purity of classical Chinese. The spoken language, also labeled "vulgar," has produced some literary monuments of its own, which were recognized as such and qualified as "classics" only a few decades ago. The unity of the two languages, classical and vernacular, which share the same fundamental structure, is undermined by grammars that are appreciably different, and by the fact that these languages hold to diametrically opposed stylistic ideals: lapidary concision on the one hand, and eloquent vigor on the other.

We conclude by pointing out that educated Chinese add to their surnames, which are always given first, a great variety of personal names, which can be disconcerting at times. The standard given name (*ming* 名)

is often avoided out of decorum; thus Tao Qian 陶潛 is often referred to by his *zi* 字 (stylename) as Tao Yuanming 陶淵明. We will retain only the best known of these names, avoiding *hao* 號 (literary name or nickname), *bie hao* 別號 (special or particular literary name), and *shi ming* 室名 (residential name) whenever possible. When other names are used, the standard *ming* will be given in parentheses.

The goal here is to enable the reader to form an idea of traditional Chinese literature, not to establish a history of it, which might result in a lengthy catalogue of works largely unknown today. We are compelled to sacrifice quantity to present a limited number of literary "stars," and to reduce the listing of their works to allow the citation of a number of previously unpublished translations, inevitably abridged but sufficient, we hope, to evoke the content of the original.

The chronological approach will be handled somewhat roughly because of the need to follow the development of the great literary genres: after the presentation of antiquity, the period in which the common culture of the educated elite was established, comes an examination of the prose genres of "high" classical literature, then the description of the art most esteemed by the literati, poetry. The final section treats the literature of diversion, the most discredited but nonetheless highly prized, which brings together the novel and the theater.

Chapter 1. Antiquity

Ancient literature, recorded by the scribes of a rapidly evolving warlike and aristocratic society, has been carefully preserved since earliest times and has become the basis of Chinese lettered culture. It is with this in mind that one must approach the evolution of literature and its role over the course of the two-thousand-year-old imperial government, which collapsed in 1911, and attempt to understand the importance (albeit increasingly limited) that ancient literature retains today.

The term "antiquity" applied to China posed no problems until certain Marxist historians went so far as to suggest that it ended only in 1919. The indigenous tradition had placed the break around 211 B.C., when political unification brought about the establishment of a centralized but "prefectural" government under the Legalists, as well as the famous burning of books opposed to the Legalist state ideology. Yet to suggest that antiquity ended so early is to minimize the contribution of Buddhism and the transformation of thought that took place between the third and seventh centuries.

The hypothesis that modernity began early, in the eleventh or perhaps twelfth century in China, was developed by Naitô Konan 内藤湖南 (1866–1934). This idea has no want of critics or of supporters. It is opposed to the accepted idea in the West, conveyed by Marxism, that China, a "living fossil," has neither entered modern times nor participated in "the global civilization" that started with the Opium War of 1840.

Nor is there unanimity concerning the periodization proposed in historical linguistics, a periodization which distinguishes Archaic Chinese of High Antiquity (from the origins of language to the third century) from Ancient Chinese of Mid-Antiquity (sixth to twelfth centuries), then Middle Chinese of the Middle Ages (thirteenth-sixteenth centuries) from Modern Chinese (seventeenth–nineteenth centuries), and Recent Chinese (1840-1919) from Contemporary Chinese (1920 to the present).

In the area of literature, the beginning of the end of antiquity could perhaps be placed in the second century A.D. Archaeology has elevated our knowledge of more ancient writings toward the beginning of the second millennium B.C., but this archaic period, discovered recently, cannot be considered part of literary patrimony in the strictest sense. Accounts of this archaic period are traditionally divided into six eras,[2] but to honor them would be to fall into the servitude of a purely chronological approach.

I. Origins

Since the last year of the last century, when Wang Yirong 王懿榮 (1845–1900) compiled the first collection of inscriptions written on bones and shells, the increasing number of archaeological discoveries has allowed the establishment of a corpus of nearly 50,000 inscriptions extending over the period from the fourteenth to the tenth centuries before our era. Dong Zuobin 董作賓 (1895–1963) proposed a periodization for them and distinguished within them the styles of different schools of scribes. Scholars have managed to decipher a third of the total of some 6,000 distinct signs, which are clearly related to the system of writing used by the Chinese today–these were certainly not primitive forms of characters.

The oracular inscriptions are necessarily short–the longest known text, of a hundred or so characters, covers the scapula of an ox and extends even over the supporting bones; the shell of a southern species of the great tortoise, also used to record divination, did not offer a more extensive surface. Whether a literature existed at this ancient time seems rather doubtful, but this scriptural evidence causes one to consider whether

---

[2]These eras are the early Chou dynasty (eleventh century–722 B.C.), the Spring and Autumn era (722–481 B.C.), the Warring States (481–256 B.C.), the Ch'in dynasty (256–206 B.C.), the Western or Early Han dynasty (206 B.C.–A.D. 6), and the Eastern or Latter Han dynasty (25–A.D. 220).

the *Shu jing* 書經 (Classic of Documents), supposedly "revised" by Confucius but often criticized as a spurious text, was based in part on authentic texts. The presence of an early sign representing a bundle of slips of wood or bamboo confirms the existence of a primitive form of book in a very ancient era–texts were written on these slips, which were then bound together to form a "fascicle."

The purpose of these ancient archives, which record the motivation for the diviner's speech, his identity, and sometimes the result, has been ignored. Of another nature are the inscriptions on bronze that appeared in about the eleventh century B.C. and went out of fashion in the second century B.C. They attracted the attention of amateur scholars from the eleventh century until modern times. Many collections of inscriptions on "stone and bronze" have been published in the intervening eras. The longest texts extend to as much as five-hundred signs, the forms of which often seem to be more archaic than those of the inscriptions on bones and shells.

The most ancient inscriptions indicate nothing more than the person to whom the bronze was consecrated or a commemoration of the name of the sponsor. Toward the tenth century B.C. the texts evolved from several dozen to as many as a hundred signs and took on a commemorative character.

The inspiration for these simple, solemn texts is not always easily discernible because of the obscurities of the archaisms in the language. An echo of certain pieces transmitted by the Confucian school can be seen in some texts, but their opacity has disheartened many generations of literati.

II. "Let a hundred flowers bloom, Let a hundred schools of thought contend!"

This statement by Mao Zedong, made to launch a liberalization movement that was cut short in 1957, was inspired by an exceptional period in Chinese cultural history (from the fifth to the third centuries

B.C.) in which there was a proliferation of schools–the "hundred schools." The various masters of these schools offered philosophical, often political, discussion. The growth of these schools paralleled the rise of rival states from the time of Confucius (the Latinized version of the Chinese original, Kong Fuzi 孔夫子 or Master Kong, ca. 551–479 B.C.) to the end of the Warring States period (221 B.C.). The "hundred schools" came to an end with the unification of China late in the third century B.C. under the Legalist rule of the Qin dynasty (221–206 B.C.). This era of freedom of thought and intellectual exchange never completely ceased to offer a model, albeit an unattainable model, in the search for an alternative to the oppressive ideology imposed by the centralized state.

Much of what has reached us from this lost world was saved in the wake of the reconstruction of Confucian writings (a subject to which we will turn shortly). The texts of the masters of the hundred schools, on the periphery of orthodox literati culture, are of uneven quality, regardless of the philosophy they offer. Even the best, however, have not come close to dethroning the "Chinese Socrates," Confucius, the first of the great thinkers, in both chronology and importance.

1. Mo Zi and the Logicians. The work known as *Mo Zi* 墨子 (Master Mo) is a collection of the writings of a sect founded by Mo Di 墨翟, an obscure personage whom scholars have wanted to make a contemporary of Confucius. It has been hypothesized that the name Mo, "ink," referred to the tattooing of a convict in antiquity, and the given name, Di, indicates the pheasant feathers that decorated the hats of the common people. Although we can only speculate about whether Mo Zi was a convict or a commoner, he argued for a kind of bellicose pacifism toward aggressors, doing his best to promote, through a utilitarian process of reasoning, the necessity of believing in the gods and of practicing universal love without discrimination. Condemning the extravagant expense of funerals as well as the uselessness of art and music, Mo Zi wrote in a style of discouraging weight. The work that has come down to us under his name (which appears to be about two-thirds of the original text) represents a direction which Chinese civilization explored without ever prizing. Mo Zi's mode of argument has influenced many generations of logicians and sophists, who are known to us only in fragments, the main contribution of which has been to demonstrate in their curious way of argumentation peculiar features of the Chinese language.

Hui Shi 惠施 is known only by the thirty-some paradoxes which the incomparable Zhuang Zi 莊子 cites, without attempting to solve, as in:

There is nothing beyond the Great Infinity. . . and the Small Infinity is not inside.

The antinomies of reason have nourished Taoist thought, if not the other way around, as Zhuang Zi attests after the death of his friend Hui Shi:

Zhuang Zi was accompanying a funeral procession. When he passed by the grave of Master Hui he turned around to say to those who were following him: "A fellow from Ying had spattered the tip of his nose with a bit of plaster, like the wing of a fly. He had it removed by [his crony] the carpenter Shi, who took his ax and twirled it around. He cut it off, then heard a wind: the plaster was entirely removed without scratching his nose. The man from Ying had remained standing, impassive. When he learned of this, Yuan, the sovereign of the country of Song, summoned the carpenter Shih and said to him, "Try then to do it again for Us." The carpenter responded, "Your servant is capable of doing it; however, the material that he made use of died long ago."

After the death of the Master, I too no longer can find the material: I no longer have anyone to talk to. (*Zhuang Zi* 24)

Sons of the logicians and the sophists, the rhetoricians shared with the Taoists a taste for apologues. They opposed the Taoist solution of a detached "non-action," involved as they were in diplomatic combat. Held in contempt by the Confucians for their "Machiavellianism," the *Zhanguo ce* 戰國策 (Intrigues of the Warring States) remains the most representative work of the genre. It was reconstructed several centuries later by Liu Xiang 劉向 (77–6 B.C.), but the authenticity of these reassembled materials seems to have been confirmed by the discovery of parallel texts in a tomb at Mawang Dui 馬王堆 in 1973. A great variety animates these accounts, both speeches and chronicles; they are rich in dialogue, which cannot be represented by this single, although characteristic, anecdote–it is inserted without commentary into the "intrigues" (or "slips") of the state of Chu:

> The King of Wei offered the King of Chu a beautiful girl who gave him great satisfaction. Knowing how much the new woman pleased him, his wife, the queen, showed her the most intense affection. She chose clothes and baubles which would please her and gave them to her; it was the same for her with rooms in the palace and bed clothes. In short, she gratified her with more attention than the king himself accorded her.
>
> He congratulated her for it: a woman serves her husband through her carnal appeal, and jealousy is her nature. Now, understanding how I love the new woman, my wife shows her more love than I–it is thus that the filial son serves his parents, that the loyal servant fulfills his duties toward his prince.
>
> As she knew that the king did not consider her jealous, the queen suggested to her rival: "The king appreciates your beauty. However, he is not that fond of your nose. You would do better to hide it when he receives you."
>
> Therefore, the new one did so when she saw His Majesty. The king asked his wife why his favorite hid her nose in his presence. She responded, "I know." "Even if it is unpleasant, tell me!" insisted the king. "She does not like your odor." "The brazen hussy!" cried the sovereign. "Her nose is to be cut off, and let no one question my order!"

The *Yan Zi chunqiu* 晏子春秋 (Springs and Autumns of Master Yen) is another reconstruction by Liu Xiang, a collection of anecdotes about Yan Ying 晏嬰, a man of small stature but great ability who was prime minister to Duke Jing 景 of Qi (547–490 B.C.)–the state that occupies what is now Shandong. Without cynicism, but full of shrewdness, these anecdotes do not lack appeal; some have often been selected as anthology pieces, of which this one is representative:

> When Master Yan was sent as an ambassador to Chu, the people of the country constructed a little gate next to the great one and invited him to enter. Yan Zi refused, declaring that it was suitable for an envoy to a country of dogs, but that it was to Chu that he had come on assignment. The chamberlain had him enter by the great gate.
>
> The King of Chu received him and said to him: "Was there then no one in Qi, for them to have sent you?" "How can you say there is no one in Qi, when there would be darkness in our capital of Linzi if the people of the three hundred quarters spread out their sleeves, and it would rain if they shook off their perspiration–so dense is the population." "But then why have you been sent?" "The practice in Qi is to dispatch a worthy envoy to a worthy sovereign; I am the most unworthy. . . ."

2. Legalism. The diplomatic manipulations and other little anecdotes we have seen in the *Yan Zi chunqiu* were of little interest to the Legalists, who took their name from the idea that the hegemonic power of the state is founded on a system of implacable laws supposing the abolition of hereditary privileges–indeed a tabula rasa that rejects morals and traditions. In fact, historians associate them with all thought that privileges efficacy. From this point of view, the most ancient "Legalist" would be the artisan of Qi's hegemony in the seventh century B.C., Guan Zi 管子 (Master Guan). The work that was handed down under his name is a composite text and in reality contains no material prior to the third century B.C. Whether or not he should be considered a Legalist, Guan Zi embodies the idea that the power of the state lies in its prosperity, and this in turn depends on the circulation of goods. In sum, Guan Zi stands for a proto-mercantilism diametrically opposed to the primitive physiocraticism of Gongsun Yang 公孫鞅 (also known as Shang Yang 商鞅), minister of Qin in the fourth century. *Shang jun shu* 商君書 (The Book of Lord Shang), which is attributed to Gongsun Yang, gives the Legalist ideas a particularly brutal form:

> It is the nature of people to measure that which is advantageous to them, to seize the best, and to draw to themselves that which is profitable. The enlightened lord must take care if he wants to establish order in his country and to be able to turn the population to his advantage, for the population has at its disposal a great number of means to avoid the strictness that it fears. Within the country he must cause the people to consecrate themselves to farming; without he must cause them to be singly devoted to warfare. This is why the order of a sage sovereign consists of multiplying interdictions in order to prevent infractions and relying on force to put an end to fraud. (*Shang jun shu*, "Suan di")

Shang Yang's prose is laden with archaisms, which hardly lighten the weight of his doctrine.

It is in the work of Han Fei Zi 韓非子 (ca. 280–233) that Legalism found its most accomplished formulation. The book *Han Fei Zi* contains a commentary on the *Classic of the Way and of Power* of Lao Zi in which the ideal of Taoist non-action is realized by the automatism of laws. The "artifice" of the latter may go back to the Confucianism of Xun Zi 荀子 (Master Xun, also known as Xun Qing 荀卿, ca. 300–230 B.C.), a school rejected by orthodox Confucianism.

Xun Zi, who happens to have been the teacher of Han Fei Zi, developed the brilliant theory that human nature inclines individuals to satisfy their egoistic appetites: it was therefore bad for advanced societies of the time. The "rites"–culture–are necessary for socialization. Xun Zi's argumentation was unprecedentedly elaborate, examining every facet of a question while avoiding repetition. In a scintillating style peppered with apologues, Han Fei Zi argues that the art of governing requires techniques other than the simple manipulation of rewards and punishments. The prince is the cornerstone of a system that is supposed to ensure him of a protective impenetrableness. The state must devote itself to eliminating the useless, noxious five "parasites" or "vermin:" the scholars, rhetoricians, knights-errant, deserters, and merchants (perhaps even artisans).

3. The Fathers of Taoism. A philosophy of evasion, this school was opposed to social and political engagement. From the outset Taoism was either a means to flee society and politics or a form of consolation for those who encountered reversals in politics and society. The poetic power of its writings, which denounced limits and aphorisms of reason, explains the fascination that it continues to hold for intellectuals educated through the rationalism of the Confucians. These works, like most of the others from antiquity that were attributed to a *master,* in fact seem to be rather disparate texts of a *school.*

The *Dao de jing* 道德經 (Classic of the Way and of Power) remains the most often translated Chinese work–and the first translated, if one counts the lost translation into Sanskrit by the monk Xuanzang 宣藏 in the seventh century A.D. This series of aphorisms is attributed to Lao Zi 老子 (Master Lao or "The Old Master"), whom tradition considers a contemporary of Confucius. He is said to have left this "testament" as he departed the Chinese world via the Xian'gu Pass for the West. In their polemics against the Buddhists, the Taoists of the following millennium used this story as the basis on which to affirm that the Buddha was none other than their Chinese Lao Zi, who had been converting the barbarians of the West since his departure from China. Modern scholarship estimates that the *Lao Zi* could not date earlier than the third century B.C. The 1973 discoveries at Mawang Dui in Hunan confirmed what scholars had suspected for centuries: the primitive *Lao Zi* is reversed in respect to ours: a *De dao jing* 德道經 (Classic of Power and the Way). Its style, which is greatly admired for its obscure concision, seems to owe much to the repair work of the commentator Wang Bi 王弼 (226–249). Thus it is tenable that the primitive *Lao Zi* was a work of military strategy. Whatever it was, the text that is preferred today runs a little over 5,000 characters and is divided into 81 sections (9 x 9). The Taoist attitude toward life is expressed here in admirably striking formulae, which lend themselves to many esoteric interpretations:

He who knows does not speak; he who speaks does not know (#56).

Govern a great state as you would fry small fish! (#60).

Practice non-action, attend to the useless, taste the flavorless. (#63)

The *Zhuang Zi* 莊子, written by Zhuang Zhou 莊周 or Zhuang Zi (Master Zhuang), was apparently abridged at about the same time as the *Lao Zi*, but at the hands of the commentator Guo Xiang 郭象 (d. 312), who cut it from fifty-two to thirty-three sections. Scholars cannot agree whether the seven initial sections, called "the inner chapters," are from the same hand of Zhuang Zhou as the sixteen following, called "the outer chapters," and the final ten "miscellaneous chapters." It is in the final ten that we find a characteristic arrangement of reconstructions from the first century, works of one school attributed to one master. In fact, it is the first part which gives the most lively impression of an encounter with an animated personality whose mind is strangely vigorous and disillusioned:

Our life is limited, but knowledge is without limit. To follow the limitless with that which is limited will exhaust one. To go unrelentingly after knowledge is exhausting and can only cause one to rush to his ruin. (*Zhuang Zi*, 3)

Great knowledge encompasses, small knowledge discriminates. Great words glitter, small words prattle. *(Zhuang Zi, 2)*

Passages and apologues familiar to every Chinese scholar abound as well in the "outer chapters:"

> Zhuang Zi was fishing with rod and line in the river Pu when two great officers sent by the King of Chu came toward him: "His majesty hopes to put you in charge of interior affairs." Without raising his line or turning his head, Zhuang Zi replied: "I have heard it said that there is a tortoise sacred to Chu, dead for three thousand years. The king has stored it away in a casket, wrapped in linen cloth, on high in the temple of his ancestors. Would it rather be dead with honors accorded to its bones or alive but dragging its tail through the mud?" The two great officers replied, "It would rather drag its tail through the mud." "Get along with you, then!" concluded Zhuang Zi. "Let me drag my tail in the mud." *(Zhuang Zi 17)*

The ideas of Zhuang Zi have sometimes been compared to nihilism:

> Master Dongguo questioned Zhuang Zi: "Where, then, is found this thing you call the Way (the Tao)?" "It is everywhere." "I am waiting for you to tell me more exactly." "In the ants." "More lowly?" "In the millet." "Still more lowly?" "In the shards of tiles." "The lowest possible?" "In shit and piss!" Master Dongguo could find no reply. *(Zhuang Zi 22)*

The work ends with a critical depiction of the "hundred schools," parallels of which are found in the *Xun Zi* and the *Han Fei Zi*. It is curious to read there an evaluation of Zhuang Zi himself, which emphasizes his sense of humor:

> He expressed himself in extravagant discourses, in strange words, in phrases without head or tail, often too freely, but without partiality, for

he did not espouse any particular point of view. The world is too
muddy to endure serious talk. . . . (*Zhuang Zi* 33)

The *Lie Zi* 列子 (Master Lie), a work divisible into 8 parts and
nearly 150 sections, is of a most heterogeneous character. Its attribution
to the legendary Lie Yukou 列禦寇, to whom chapter 32 of the *Zhuang Zi*
is consecrated, is not worthy of serious consideration. It is no less than a
treasury of well-known apologues, perhaps of a popular nature, such as
that of "the faith that raised mountains" (see part five, section three), a
modern version of which was propagated by Mao Zedong.

A number of other schools have left nothing but allusions or
fragmentary descriptions which can be discovered in the writings of their
adversaries, such as–thanks to Mencius–the anarchists who refused to
exploit the work of others and, so it is said, produced everything with
their own hands. Neither the one nor the other was much concerned
with literature in the pure sense. The triumph of the Confucian school,
which was most violently persecuted during the ephemeral Legalist reign
of the Qin (221–206 B.C.), can be explained by political, moral, and
social reasons. The scholarly doctrine, however, has expanded its empire
only progressively, and not without fits and starts. It was the examination
system, instituted in the seventh century A.D., that made the Confucian
school the official ideology of the state. But the work of reconstructing a
worn-out tradition was energized from the second century B.C. by the
sort of literary influence exercised by these Confucian texts on all cultivated
spirits in China for more than two thousand years.

III. The Confucian Classics

The word *jing* 經 means the warp of a fabric: on the woof of the
Confucian Classics is woven the cultural unity of China. The same term
designates the Buddhist sutras, later the "Marxist Classics."

With an impetus from Confucius, the school seems to have assumed
from the outset the role of transmitter of The Tradition. The "Six Classics"

are mentioned in the *Zhuang Zi*. Over the passage of time, the classics grew in number to seven, nine, twelve, and finally thirteen.

The *Yi jing* 易經 (Classic of Changes), the only work that was not proscribed by the First Emperor of Qin (r. 221–210 B.C.), is unique; it is first a book of divination, the "bible" of a binary method that permits the construction of sixty-four hexagrams derived from the eight basic trigrams. The first paragraph following each hexagram, the *tuan* 彖 (verdict), reveals the network of meanings; the *yao* 爻, a second paragraph, explains each of the lines of the hexagram, full or broken–this is the technical part, which appeared toward the end of the second millennium B.C., tradition assures us, but only in the seventh or eighth century A.D. according to modern scholarship. Numerous philosophical or divinatory glosses have been incorporated into it. It has added "ten wings," certain commentaries in which have been attributed to Confucius himself. In these "wings," which were certainly later additions, metaphysical considerations of a profound obscurity are sometimes developed. The work has fascinated a number of scholars who have been able to satisfy their taste for mystery in it without deserting orthodoxy.

The documents preserved in the *Shu jing* 書經, translated by James Legge (1815–1897) under the title *The Book of Historical Documents*, are similarly dated to the eleventh to seventh centuries B.C. The book is a collection of memorable speeches, discourses, harangues, and instructions, arranged in chronological order. The extant text is the version written in ancient-style characters in fifty chapters, of which twenty-two are forgeries dating from the third or fourth century B.C.

The *Chun qiu* 春秋 (Spring and Autumn) is a chronicle of the years 722 to 481 B.C. in the state of Lu, where Confucius lived. Although this book is written in an extraordinarily laconic style, Confucius is said to have hidden his judgments in it through the subtle choice of words. Two commentaries, *Gongyang zhuan* 公羊傳 and *Guliang zhuan* 穀梁傳, are said to have been written by individuals named Gongyang and Guliang respectively, about whom little else is known; they endeavor to show the positive or negative values in these judgments. The glosses in these two works appear to date to the third century B.C. The third commentary, attributed to Zuo Qiuming 左邱明 and titled *Zuo zhuan* 左傳, appears to be older. Each of these commentaries is considered a classic. The *Zuo zhuan,* translated with the *Chun qiu* under the title *Spring and Autumn Annals and Tso chuan* by James Legge, often has only the most distant relationship to the text upon which it comments and is probably composed of fragments of chronicles of other kingdoms, of a fantastic prolixity compared to the dryness of the *Chun qiu* chronicle itself.

Thus the simple mention of the death of a prince of Qi in the eleventh month of the twenty-third year of the reign of Duke Xi 僖 of Lu (636 B.C.) provides an occasion, following a brief formal commentary, to retrace at length the career of Chong'er 重耳, exiled son of Duke Xian 獻, the ruler of the state of Jin. A dispute with his wives occupies a considerable part of this account–here is an episode:

> The Earl of Qin gave five women to him [Chong'er], among them Ying [widow of Yu of Jin, posthumously Duke] of Huai. When she presented him with a pitcher to wash his hands and rinse his mouth, he signaled to her [to retire] when he had finished [with his hands still wet]. Indignant, she angrily said, "Qin and Jin are states of the same rank. Why do you treat me in this contemptuous fashion?" The son of the duke was so afraid that he took off his clothes and put on the garb of a prisoner.

Traits common to the majority of these anecdotes are the importance attached to the rites which governed the "civilized" peoples of the Early Chou dynasty states and the warfare so often recalled by the *Zuo zhuan.*

The reconstruction of three ritual books, each of a quite different character, can be attributed to the Confucian school. Together they constitute a systematic description of the social and political organization of the upper classes in ancient society.

The *Zhou li* 周禮, translated by Edouard Biot in 1851 under the title *Rites des Tcheou* (Rites of Zhou), is a systematic description of an ideal administration, or at least it has been so judged by generations of reformers of the imperial regime in search of a utopian model.

The *Yi li* 儀禮 (rendered as the *Book of Etiquette and Ceremonial* in the 1917 translation by John Steele) is the only one of these three "ritual books" which merits that label from cover to cover. Completely different as well from a work such as *Leviticus,* this book, which is divided into twenty-seven chapters, describes in detail the ceremonies that punctuated the life of the noble houses. This system of rules presented in a series of narratives does not seem to go back beyond the third century B.C., although it does include some older material. A concern for detail is evident here that presages the Chinese novelists of some two-thousand years later. Rules of savoir-faire are expressed with a wealth of impressive detail.

The *Li ji* 禮記, translated by James Legge in 1885 (Oxford: Clarendon) under the title *Book of Rites,* is a composite work nearly three times the size of the *Yi li.* Its forty-six chapters are the result of an abridgment of a primitive collection by Dai 戴 the Elder, a little-known figure. In the first century B.C., Dai combined eighty-five treatises on ritual. Dai the Younger, a cousin, extracted from this a work of forty-six treatises, three of which differ from our current text of the *Li ji,* which was edited and reshaped in the second century A.D.

The principal interest of the *Li ji* is clearly not literary, but it nevertheless occupies a place in literary history for having provided two of the *Four Books* or *Si shu* 四書. These texts have been the foundation of Chinese primary education since the fourteenth century. At the same time, they were popular books and forbidding texts to their youthful, semiliterate readers. The first of the *Four Books,* which was edited by the eminent scholar and Neo-Confucian philosopher Zhu Xi 朱熹 (1130–1200), is essentially the treatise that appears as chapter 39 of the *Li ji,* the *Da xue* 大學 or *Grand Study,* that is to say, what adults were intended to study (according to Zhu Xi's interpretation). The text developed a typically

Confucian reasoning in the form of a sorites, of which the second and third part, where "things and beings are examined," depict Confucius as similar to a defender of the natural sciences in the nineteenth century.

> Those [of the princes] from the past who wished to make their virtue shine brightly under heaven, began by ordering the reigns in their own states. Whoever wished to order the reign of his own state, began by harmonizing his family. Whoever wished to harmonize his family, began by cultivating his person. Whoever wished to cultivate his person, began by rectifying his heart and his spirit. Whoever wished to rectify his heart and his spirit, began by making his will sincere. Whoever wished to make his will sincere, first set out to perfect his knowledge.
>
> Perfecting one's knowledge consists in investigating things and beings.
>
> It is only after investigating things and beings that knowledge is perfected. It is only when knowledge is perfected that the will is sincere. It is only when the will is sincere that the heart and spirit are rectified . . . [thus it follows until the conclusion]. It is only when the state is well governed that the world is at peace. From the Son of Heaven to the common people, all should apply themselves to cultivating their persons.

The second of the *Four Books* comes from chapter 28 of the *Li ji*. It is entitled *Zhong yong* 中庸, translated by James Legge as the *Doctrine of the Mean*. Legge's translation is based on the inspired commentary of Zhu Xi and returns in the text to the most ancient interpretation of the "true Mean." The *Zhong yong* abounds in allusions and citations taken from the other Confucian classics, in particular from the poetry of the *Shi jing,* to which we will soon return.

The third of the *Four Books,* the *Analects of Confucius* or the *Lunyu* 論語 (Words [of the Master] Arranged in Order), is the most prestigious of the Confucian Classics, revered in all of East Asia. Here Confucius speaks to us in person (although he is referred to simply as "the Master"); thus, it is not excessive to see a parallel to the Gospels, even though traditional

Chinese critics have shown that the collection could not have been put together until a generation or more after the Master died, and that the last five of its "books" are of a separate origin. Although these "texts" were probably passed on orally at first, different versions were recorded in different states; the version used today was established only in the third century A.D., based on the edition from the state of Lu (the editors taking into consideration two others versions, that of the state of Qi and that in ancient-style characters). The Confucius that one discovers in the *Analects* inspired enthusiasm among the rationalist philosophers of the Enlightenment era in the West. Though he is the patron of the orthodox doctrines of Chinese imperial regimes, Confucius expresses in this book a grassroots wisdom, offered in lively dialogues, which gives substance to the atheism shared by the majority of Chinese scholars throughout history. The famous response of the Master to Zilu is dictated only by his concern for consecrating his teachings to the conduct his disciples ought to follow in order to serve mankind in serving the state, as a benevolent ruler, not a tyrant:

> (XI, 12) Asked by Zilu about the service of the gods and demons, the Master replied, "How can one be adept in this, when one still doesn't know how to serve man?"
> "Can I question you about death?"
> "How could I, still not understanding life, know of death?"

Confucius advocated modesty rather than agnosticism:

> (II, 17) The Master said, "Zilu, I am going to teach you what it is to know. To know is to know what you know and what you do not know. This is knowledge!"

Posterity has exalted Confucius to the point of making him a *shengren* 聖人, a term without religious implications that could be translated as "saint." He did not speak of this himself:

(VII, 26) A "saint" I have not had the good fortune to see. It would be good enough to encounter an "honest man."

(VII, 34) As for the question of "saintliness" or "goodness," how can I claim them? The most that can be said is that I apply myself to them without lassitude, teach them without tiring.

"Goodness," *ren* 仁, is the cardinal virtue advocated by Confucius. It has been argued that it is best translated by "altruism," "humanity," or, very simply, "virtue." The moral ideal is that of the "son of the sovereign or lord," *junzi* 君子. Legge's rendering of this term as "gentleman" has been followed by most English translators.

The "petty man," *xiaoren* 小人, is the *junzi*'s opposite.

There is no more happy formula illustrating the position of Confucius than the following:

(VIII, 13) If the world follows the good Way, show yourself; if not, hide yourself. If it is shameful to live in poverty and scorn in a country following the good Way; to be rich and honored in an inhumane country is even more so.

But he rejects the extreme inferences that are drawn from the ideas of the hermits, one of whom, Jieni, talks with Zilu here as he hoes his garden:

(XVIII, 6). . . "The world is everywhere carried along by a wave so powerful that nothing can change its course. Rather than follow a scholar who keeps fleeing from men [i.e., Confucius], wouldn't it be better to follow someone who flees from the world?" Jieni responded to Zilu without ceasing to hoe.

The disciple reported his words to Confucius, who sighed and said: "One doesn't know how to flock with the birds and beasts. With whom else should I associate if I give up the company of men? If the world had the Way, I would not seek to change it."

Not that the "goodness" of the Master did not extend beyond mankind:

> (VII, 27) The Master fished with a line, but never with a net. He
> did not shoot at perching birds.

The last of the *Four Books* contains the words of Meng Zi 孟子
(Master Meng, ca. 390–305 B.C.), who is better known by his Latinized
title of Mencius; this work was also the last (seventh century A.D.) to be
considered part of the corpus of thirteen works known as the Confucian
Classics. The *Meng Zi* is the only text to have been temporarily excluded
from the classics after it had become a part of the corpus–in the fourteenth
century it was banned for a time, because it held that in some cases
tyrannicide was justified:

> (I.B.8) King Xuan of Qi asked: "Is a subject allowed to assassinate
> his sovereign?"
> "He who robs 'goodness,' I call a robber. He who violates the
> moral, I call a violator. A robber or a violator is only an ordinary
> person. I have heard tell of the punishment inflicted on the tyrant Zhou,
> an ordinary person, not of the murder of a sovereign."

The text of Mencius is probably the most ancient of the philosophic
works. Its style, devoid of archaisms, is supple in the lively discourses
presented in the form of dialogues, and its argumentation is sustained by
the colorful comparisons:

> (VI.A.1) "Human nature," Gao Zi responded, "is like swirling water.
> If a passage is opened for it to the east, it rushes there. But it could flow
> out as well to the west, if a passage were opened to the west. Human
> nature does not distinguish good and evil."
> Mencius replied, "Water indeed does not distinguish east from west,
> but is it the same for high and low? Human nature seeks the good as
> water heads for a low point. There is no man who would not be good,

no water that would not flow downward. Of course, if it is struck, water will splash higher than the forehead, if it is forced, it will climb hills. But is this the nature of water? It adapts itself to circumstances. The same is true when men are pushed to evil."

Completely different from the *Analects* in its style, the *Mencius* is no less tied to the richness of ideas which Mencius's master Confucius had treated, but they are often examined in greater depth here.

There are only three more classics in the thirteen of the standard edition titled *Shisan jing zhushu* 十三經注疏 (The Thirteen Classics Commented and Expanded Upon). The first of these is the *Xiao jing* 孝經 (Classic of Filial Piety), a relatively late pamphlet which does not have much more literary importance than the second of this trio, the *Er ya* 爾 雅, a lexicon that classifies words into nineteen categories and can be considered the most ancient Chinese dictionary extant today.

Remaining to be discussed is the most important of the classics from a literary point of view, the *Shi jing* 詩經 (Classic of Poetry). The 305 poems in this anthology were said to have been chosen by Confucius from among more than 3,000. The standard version, which is also the only complete text to have reached us, includes a commentary of moral and political interpretations attributed to a certain Mao Heng 毛亨 in the third century B.C. The edition is said to have been transcribed by Liu Xin 劉歆 (50 B.C.–23 A.D.), one of the most ardent defenders of the classics in ancient characters. The anthology contains pieces of greatly differing dates and genres, stretching, according to certain critics, from the twelfth to the fifth centuries B.C., and including odes, hymns, and love songs. Love is the theme of the first poem in the collection (here the rendering is based on the French of Marcel Granet's *Festivals and Songs of Ancient China [Fêtes et chansons anciennes de la Chine]*, 1911); the interpretation here goes back to that of Zhu Xi (1130–1200), who later became the paragon of orthodoxy:

The Ospreys
In harmony the ospreys cry / In the river, on the rocks.
The maiden goes into retirement, / A fit mate for the prince.

Long or short the duck-weed: / To the left and right let us seek it.
The maiden goes into retirement, / Day and night let us ask for her.
Ask for her. . . useless quest. . . / Day and night let us think of her.
Ah! what pain! Ah! what pain! / This way and that we toss and turn.

Long or short the duck-weed: / To the left and right let us take it.
The maiden goes into retirement, / Guitars and lutes welcome her!

Long or short the duck-weed: / To the left and right let us gather it.
The maiden goes into retirement, / Bells and drums welcome her!

The 160 poems in the section devoted to the "airs of the [fifteen] states,"
guofeng 國風, preserve for the most part a popular, oral tradition, which
also seems to be the case for the "lesser odes," *xiao ya* 小雅 (numbers
161–234), songs of minor celebrations. The "greater odes," *da ya* 大雅
(nos. 235–265), celebrate the major occasions, particularly the
accompanying war dances. The hymns, *song* 頌 (nos. 266–305), seem to
have been part of religious rituals.

Repetition, refrain, rhythm, and assonance are the common
characteristics of popular songs throughout the world. They also mark
the three hundred poems in this collection, and are sometimes still
perceptible when the poems are recited in modern Chinese pronunciation.
Recourse to metaphorical evocation, *xing* 興, or the comparisons drawn
from nature, *bi* 比, and the description, *fu* 賦, in some of the prestigious
poems, introduce some processes recognized as fundamental in the Chinese
prosodic tradition.

But the *Classic of Poetry,* which bookish scholars in subsequent
centuries sometimes regarded as primarily a means of enriching their
vocabulary of flora and fauna, played a completely different role in

antiquity. Filled with moral and political allusions, it was a treasure-trove of much of the culture common to the Chinese "confederation" and was often cited by gentlemen in ancient times to make a political point. Confucius, in fact, was already emphasizing the double role of the *Classic of Poetry* as both a literary and a diplomatic sourcebook in the *Analects:*

> (XVII, 9) My children, why do you neglect studying the Poems? The Poems will allow you to stimulate, allow you to observe, allow you to keep company, allow you to protest. . . . And you will learn there the names of a good number of birds, beasts, plants, and trees.

> (XVI, 13) Chen Kang asked the son of Confucius if his father had given him special instructions.
> "No. One time when I found him alone and I was hurrying across the courtyard, he asked me if I had studied the Poems. 'Not yet,' I responded. 'Without studying them, you will not know how to express yourself.'"

We are assured that Confucius did his best to cite the Poems without recourse to his dialectal pronunciation, as if the Master was already aware that he was transmitting a common cultural fund. With the glosses and regulation commentaries, the thirteen classics, *Yi jing, Shu jing, Shi jing, Zhou li, Yi li, Li ji, Chun qiu–Zuo zhuan, Gongyang zhuan, Guliang zhuan, Xiao jing, Lunyu, Meng Zi,* and *Er ya,* total nearly six million characters; the texts themselves, which every candidate for the civil service examinations after the fourteenth century had to know by heart, contain nearly a half-million words–the basis of a literary training that should not be underestimated.

Suggested Further Reading

A number of on-line resources of relevance can be found by consulting
the Association for Asian Studies "Asia Resources on the World Wide
Web" (http://www.aasianst.org/asiawww.htm) and the Internet Guide for
Chinese Studies, World-Wide Web Virtual Library sponsored by Australia
National University and Heidelberg University (http://sun.sino.uni-
heidelberg.de/igcs). The appropriate sections of *Sources of Chinese Tradition,*
ed. William Theodore de Bary and Irene Bloom (2nd ed., New York:
Columbia University Press, 1998), are also highly recommended. *Indiana
Companion* in the entries below refers to *The Indiana Companion to Traditional
Chinese Literature,* volumes 1 and 2 (Bloomington: Indiana University
press, 1986 and 1998).

Antiquity
Ho, Ping-ti. *The Cradle of the East.* Chicago: University of Chicago Press,
    1975.
Hsü, Cho-yun. *Ancient China in Transition.* Stanford: Stanford University
    Press, 1965.
Keightley, David N. *The Origins of Chinese Civilization.* Berkeley: University
    of California Press, 1983.
Maspero, Henri. *China in Antiquity.* Frank A. Kierman, trans. Amherst:
    University of Massachusetts Press, 1978. Although sections are
    dated, this is a good, basic introduction.
Watson, Burton. *Early Chinese Literature.* New York: Columbia University
    Press, 1962.

The Hundred Schools of Thought
Ames, Roger, trans. *Sun-tzu: The Art of Warfare.* New York: Ballantine
    Books, 1993.

"Chuang Tzu." In *Indiana Companion,* II: 20–26.

"Chu–tzu pai–chia" (The Various Masters and the Hundred Schools). In *Indiana Companion,* I: 336–343.

Henricks, Robert, trans. *Lao Tzu, Te–Tao Ching.* New York: Ballantine Books, 1990.

Knoblock, John, trans. *Xunzi: A Translation and Study of the Complete Works.* 3 vols. Stanford: Stanford University Press, 1988, 12990, 1994.

Lafargue, Michael. *Tao and Method, A Reasoned Approach to the Tao Te Ching.* Albany: SUNY Press, 1994.

Lau, D. C., trans. *Lao Tzu-Tao Te Ching.* Harmondsworth: Penguin, 1963.

LeBlanc, Charles. *Huai-Nan Tzu: Philosophical Synthesis in Early Han Thought.* Hong Kong: Hong Kong University Press, 1985.

Lundahl, Bertil. *Han Fei Zi, the Man and the World.* Vol. 4. Stockholm East Asian Monographs, Stockholm: Institute of Oriental Languages, 1992.

Mair, Victor H., trans. *Lao Tzu, Tao Te Ching: The Classic Book of Integrity and the Way-An Entirely New Translation Based on the Recently Discovered Ma–wang–tui Manuscripts.* New York: Bantam Books, 1990.

Major, John S., trans. *Heaven and Earth in Early Han Thought: Chapters Three, Four, and Five of the Huainanzi.* Albany: SUNY Press, 1993.

Rickett, W. Allyn, trans. *Guanzi: Political, Economic and Philosophical Essays from Early China-A Study and Translation.* 2 vols. Princeton: Princeton University Press, 1985 and 1997.

Waley, Arthur, trans. *The Way and Its Power.* New York: Macmillan, 1934.

Watson, Burton, trans. *Chuang tzu.* New York: Columbia University Press, 1968.

___. *Basic Writings of Mo tzu, Hsün tzu, and Han–fei tzu.* New York: Columbia University Press, 1967.

The Confucian Classics

Brooks, E. Bruce, with A. Taeko Brooks. *The Original Analects: Sayings of Confucius and His Successors.* New York: Columbia University Press, 1998.

"Ching" (Classics). In *Indiana Companion,* I: 309–316.

Huang, Chichung. *The Analects of Confucius: A Literal Translation with an Introduction and Notes.* Oxford: Oxford University Press, 1997.

Karlgren, Bernhard, trans. *The Book of Odes.* Stockholm: Museum of Far Eastern Antiquities, 1950.

Lau, D. C., trans. *The Analects.* Penguin: Harmondsworth, 1979.

Legge, James, trans. *The Chinese Classics.* Oxford: Clarendon Press, 1893–1895.

Loewe, Michael. *Early Chinese Texts: A Bibliographic Guide.* Berkeley: The Society for the Study of Early China and the Institute of East Asian Studies, University of California, Berkeley, 1993.

Lynn, Richard John, trans. *The Classic of Changes: A New Translation of the I Ching as Interpreted by Wang Bi.* New York: Columbia University Press, 1994.

Shaughnessy, Edward L. *Before Confucius: Studies in the Creation of the Chinese Classics.* Albany: SUNY Press, 1997.

"Shih ching" (Classic of Poetry). In *Indiana Companion,* I: 692–694.

"Tso chuan" (Tso Documentary). In *Indiana Companion,* I: 804–806.

Waley, Arthur, trans. *The Analects of Confucius.* London: Allen and Unwin, 1938.

___. *The Book of Songs.* London: Allen and Unwin, 1937.

Watson, Burton, trans. *The Tso Chuan: Selections from China's Oldest Narrative History.* New York: Columbia University Press, 1992.

Chapter 2. Prose

"If poetry is intended to express the sentiments and the will while communicating the emotions, the role of prose is to communicate ideas, nothing more." Such a literary doctrine could be extracted from the texts transmitted by or commented on by Confucius. This utilitarian conception of literature in the service of morality would be called into question in the third century A.D. when the imperial unity of the Han dynasty disintegrated into a number of statelets, a time that has come to be called the Period of Disunion (180–589 A.D.). Was this a coincidence?

The same word, *wen* 文, the sense of which has evolved from "writing" to "literature," can also mean "ornate" or "refined." *Wen* in this latter sense was juxtaposed to *zhi* 質, "substance" or "substantial," to become the two lines of opposing force in traditional literary criticism. But *wen* in a restricted sense has come to designate prose dedicated to the simplicity of the "substantial," in opposition to poetry, *shi* 詩, which was of necessity "ornate."

Literary realities respond only imperfectly to this scheme. The frontiers that separate the two great domains of prose and poetry are poorly defined. Rhythm, normally associated with poetry, is essential to artistic prose. Rhyme and assonance are also not limited to verse. The genres in parallel prose–*pian wen* 駢文, woven with literary allusions, or the *fu* 賦 (rhapsody or prose-poem), a descriptive evocation in rhythmic prose–are closer to poetry, distinguished from it only by the priority accorded the container over the contents.

To translate such texts, which are overloaded with "ornamentation," and even more to appreciate them, is nearly impossible. They are truly accessible only to the disappearing breed of scholars who have had a traditional-style education. The same is true for all of the "mandarin genres"–dissertations, tributes, judgments and other occasional works which are abundantly represented in the anthologies and collected works of individual authors. Because of the huge number of such works that have been written over the centuries, only a very incomplete picture of these genres can be presented, with preference given to those which remain "classical," that is to say, those which are taught in the schools and read by the public at large in annotated editions often paired with versions "translated" into modern Chinese.

This seems an ideal place to mention the importance of the anthologies that followed one after the other from the third century A.D. until modern times, each piece in which was selected because of its literary brilliance. The most ancient, that by Du Yu 杜預 (222–284), has been lost, eclipsed by the *Wen xuan* 文選 (A Selection of Literature) compiled by Xiao Tong 蕭統 (501–531), a work which for a long time provided many of the texts memorized by mandarins for the examination competition, and which served as a model for the many anthologies that included both prose and poetry. The *Guwenci leizuan* 古文辭類纂 (Collection by Category of Ancient Prose and Poetry), compiled in 1799 by Yao Nai 姚鼐 (1732–1815), and its sequels were enormously successful with scholars. Together they constitute the finest texts of classical Chinese prose of the last two millennia, with representative poetic genres also included.

It was the twelfth century before the first anthologies devoted exclusively to prose appeared; the pieces they contained were called *sanwen* 散文, "free" or "dispersed prose," in contrast to the prosodic regulations of *pianwen* 騈文, "parallel" or "harnessed prose." The *Songwen jian* 宋文鑑 (Mirror of Song Prose), for example, by Lü Zuqian 呂祖謙 (1137–1181), is a collection of the best pieces produced by Song-dynasty authors (960–1279) during the first two centuries of the Song reign. For the Ming dynasty (1368–1644), the most important collection is the anthology compiled by Huang Zongxi 黃宗羲 (1610–1695), the *Mingwen hai* 明文海 (The Ocean of Ming Prose). The most popular of the anthologies remaining today was published in 1695 by two cousins named Wu Chucai

吳楚材 and Wu Diaohou 吳調侯; the *Guwen guanzhi* 古文觀止 (The Major
Works of Ancient Prose), is a limited selection of 220 extracts, of which,
next to the excerpts from Zuo's commentary to the *Chun qiu*, the work
most often cited is Sima Qian's *Shi ji*.

I. Narrative Art and Historical Records

Besides the Zuo commentary to the *Chun qiu*, other narrative texts
dating from a time later than the burning of the books in 213 B.C. have
come down to us. Among them are texts which have been labeled early
novels by some modern critics, despite the lack of support for this
classification in traditional assessments. One such book is the *Mu Tianzi
zhuan* 穆天子傳 (Chronicle of the Son of Heaven Mu), which was discovered
in a tomb in A.D. 279, and which relates the fantastic voyages of its hero.

Many factors ensure these narrative texts an important place in the
history of belles lettres. First, to a certain extent they fill the void caused
by the lack of an epic in Chinese literature. Second, a number of eminent
writers participated in the compilation of these historical works or had
their own pieces included in them. Most often these included pieces were
judgments or elegies, many of which have become widely regarded as
major works of classical Chinese prose. Finally, and most important, the
outstanding model for reconstructing the history of an imperial regime is
a work that has fascinated scholars in the two thousand years since it was
written.

This work is the *Shi ji* 史記 (Records of the Grand Historian),
written by China's Herodotus, Sima Qian 司馬遷 (ca. 145–ca. 85 B.C.).
Sima Qian, however, was able to produce a work quite different from its
obvious Greek counterparts. The *Shi ji* offers an original organization of
Sima Qian's material, which was nothing less than the history of the
world as it was then known. After twelve "basic annals," dedicated to the
dynasties of earlier times and the emperors of the more recent Qin and
Han dynasties, there are ten "chronological tables," eight "monographs,"
thirty chapters on the "hereditary houses" (including the "house of

Confucius"), and finally seventy "biographies." Perhaps one should credit this arrangement to Sima Tan 司馬談 (d. 110 B.C.), the father of the Grand Historian who began this great enterprise–or blame him, because the material about one man or one event is often scattered through several chapters, and because the treatment of some men and events lacks balance. Allowing for some reorganization, however, this was the structure followed by all the subsequent official dynastic histories, most of which after the fifth century A.D. were mostly compiled by bureaus of history and are thereby devoid of personality.

What Chinese scholars have read between the lines in Sima Qian's history is a deep resentment of imperial tyranny–in 99 B.C. he was sentenced to be castrated for lese majesty in the defense of his friend, the general Li Ling 李陵, who was guilty of having allowed himself to be captured alive by the barbarian Xiongnu. The reader appreciates in Sima Qian's historical accounts, and in the subtle arrangement of the stories, a resistance masked by a resonant restraint, and a talent for storytelling that masterfully combines discourse and narrative.

Thus Xiang Yu 項羽, the unlucky rival of Liu Bang 劉邦, who founded the Han dynasty under which Sima Qian lived, was given a "basic annals" although he never ruled the empire. The passage recounting the final battle between Xiang Yu and Liu Bang at Gaixia and the pathos of Xiang Yu's last stand are particularly celebrated accounts, repeated in the theater and in a number of other popular genres.

The historian's "elegy" that closes the long biographical account of Xiang Yu is a piece fit for an anthology:

> I have heard Master Zhou say that Shun [our model emperor] has eyes with double pupils, and I have also heard that Xiang Yu had eyes with double pupils. Could it be that Xiang Yu was his descendant? How sudden was his rise! When Qin lost control of the government, Chen She was the first to cause difficulties, and men of power and distinction rose like a swarm of wasps, struggling with each other in numbers too

great to count. Xiang Yu, without even an inch of territory, took advantage
of the situation and rose in arms from the farming fields. Within three
years he led the five feudal lords to annihilate Qin, divide up the world,
and enfeoff kings and marquises. All political power emanated from
Xiang Yu, who proclaimed himself Hegemon King. Even though he
was unable to hold this position until the end, his deeds are unprecedented.
Then Xiang Yu turned his back on the "land within the Passes" to
embrace Chu. He banished the Righteous emperor and enthroned
himself, full of resentment for the feudal lords rebelling against him.
What difficulties he put himself in! He made a show of his own knowledge,
never learning from the ancients. He called his enterprise that of a
Hegemon King, intending to manage the world by means of mighty
campaigns. After five years he finally lost his state. Even when he died
alone at Dongcheng, he did not come to his senses and blame himself.
What error! To excuse himself by claiming "Heaven destroyed me, it
was not any fault of mine in employing troops." Is this not madness?

The pathos of the storyteller Sima Qian reappears in many of the
biographies in the final seventy chapters of the *Records of the Grand Historian*.
It also figures notably in the chapters devoted to foreign countries or
peoples. The most remarkable example is the treatment of minor figures
in collective biographies under labels such as "The Harsh Officials,"
"The Redressers of Wrongs," and "Favorites and Minions." There has
never been a Chinese historian who was not also very nearly a novelist.
This can be clearly seen in one of the biographies collected in the chapter
on assassins, which recounts Jing Ke's near-assassination of the future
First Emperor of Qin (r. 221–210 B.C.) in 227 B.C.

The *Records of the Grand Historian* also made room for the comedians
who often played the role of jester for the princes, masking their criticisms
with witty remarks. The historian's preface to the chapter on jesters justifies
the inclusion of such a chapter:

"The Six Classics," said Confucius, "aim at the same goal–to govern well. The *(Classic of) Ritual* is employed to control the people, the *(Classic of) Music* works toward developing harmony, the *(Classic of) Documents* works toward guiding affairs of state, the *(Classic of) Poetry* works toward expressing one's ideas, the *(Classic of) Changes* works toward uplifting the soul, and the chronicle of *Spring and Autumn* works toward righteousness." "Vast is the Way of Heaven," said the Grand Astrologer (and chronicler, Sima Tan, father of Sima Qian). "Isn't it huge? And yet the 'trifling words' [of the jesters] can sometimes hit the mark."

No document is as revealing of Sima Qian's personality as his "Letter in Reply to Ren An," one of the most famous works of the epistolary genre, a vehicle used by the most eminent writers in China to address serious subjects, often for an intended audience far beyond a single addressee:

It is not easy to explain the affair [that led to my castration] to ordinary people point by point. My father did not reach the stage of holding the seals and investitures of a high dignitary. Chronicles and the calendar placed him close to fortune-tellers, among those with whom the sovereign took his pleasure–the comedians whom he nourished and whom the common people hold in contempt. If I had submitted to the law and suffered execution, it would have made no more difference than the loss of a hair from a herd of cows, no more difference than the death of an ant. The world would not compare me with those who died to retain their honor; it would simply consider that, having exhausted every clever method, I would not be able to escape from the enormity of my crime and that in the end I had no choice but to die. Why is this? It is so because of the modesty of the position I had established myself in. Every man assuredly has only a single death. A death is sometimes more weighty than Mount Tai, sometimes lighter than a goose feather–the difference lies in the use to which it is put. . . .

Lacking the power to make their concept of the Way prevail, let all these authors report the events of the past while thinking about their posterity. . . . Before my draft was completed, I was struck by misfortune. Regretting that it was incomplete caused me to confront without indignation the most ignominious of tortures. If I truly get to finish writing it, it will be hidden in a "famous mountain" and handed on to those who will appreciate it, so that it can be spread throughout the cities and the capital, at once atoning for the disgrace of my humiliation. Even were I to suffer ten thousand humiliations, how could I feel regret [as long as I complete my history]! But this can only be said to those who understand [the situation]. It is difficult to make a common person understand.

Although few, if any, Chinese women left letters, the epistolary genre was one of the most open, allowing the writer to broach all subjects, from the most serious to the most intimate.

The famous painter of bamboo Zheng Xie 鄭燮 (best known by his *hao* Banqiao 板橋, 1693–1765) left a series of famous letters addressed to his younger brother:

Having been able to have a son only at age fifty two, how could I not love him? It is rather a question of loving him in a good way. Even in games and amusements it is necessary to make him honest and kindly, to prevent him from being cruel and irascible. There is nothing in life which displeases me as much as keeping birds in a cage. We look for pleasure while they are in prison. What is the point of vexing the nature of these creatures to please our own? As for tying a dragonfly to a hair or attaching a thread to a crab to make a plaything for a child, this is merely to condemn them to be mutilated and die in a moment. Heaven and earth have begot these creatures, transformed and nourished them with great effort. . . . The Emperor on High also cherishes them with his heart. But if we men, who are the most noble of creatures, are incapable of embodying the compassionate heart of Heaven, on whom can the ten thousand creatures rely?

II. The Return of the "Ancient Style"

"Family instruction manuals" were written in the style of letters to
the family. The most representative of these works is by Yan Zhitui 顏之
推 (531–ca. 590). The simplicity of the style of his *Yanshi jiaxun* 顏氏家訓
(Family Instructions for the Yan Clan) heralded the return of "ancient-style
prose," which modern critics have made into a "movement," *guwen yundong*
古文運動 (the ancient-prose movement). This work, divided into twenty
sections, is comprehensive, illustrating its advice with anecdotes and
adopting a personal tone. It begins with the education of children, which
is deemed indispensable for everyone but prodigies, who can be excused
from it, and morons, who would not profit from it.

Yan Zhitui, who proclaimed the necessity of faith, devoted an
entire section to the defense and illustration of the doctrines of Sâkyamuni,
who, according to Yan, perfected the ideas of Confucius. This was in
marked contrast to the opinions espoused by Han Yu 韓愈 (768–824),
the first advocate to call for a return to ancient-style prose. Han was one
of the forerunners of a philosophical movement known as Neo-
Confucianism that blossomed in the eleventh and twelfth centuries, and
he was violently hostile to Buddhism, which in his eyes was as useless as
Taoism, but with the added detriment of having barbarian origins.

The principal argument of the report that Han Yu submitted to
Emperor Xianzong (r. 806–820) in 819, reproaching him for honoring a
relic of the Buddha, reads as follows:

> I hear that Your Majesty has ordered Buddhist monks to accompany
> a [finger-joint] bone of the Buddha from Fengxiang, and that you aim to
> observe the procession which will bring the relic into the palace from a
> tower. Further, orders have been given to all the monasteries to go in
> succession and offer sacrifices to it. While I am only your ignorant
> servant, I am convinced that Your Majesty neither has been beguiled
> by the Buddha nor would worship him in order to seek blessings, but
> that [this celebration] is because of the joy among the people at the

plentiful harvest. Your Majesty is complying with the people's heartfelt wishes to set up this unusual spectacle for the populace of the capital as a means of amusement. How could such a sage, enlightened ruler believe in such affairs?

However, the common people are ignorant, easy to beguile and difficult to enlighten. If they see Your Majesty act like this, they will say that you are serving the Buddha with a sincere devotion. . . . For Buddha was originally a barbarian who did not speak the languages of China; nor was his dress similar to ours.

If the Buddha were still alive today, and had received the orders of his state to come to the capital as an envoy to court, and Your Majesty would have granted to receive him, it would be by no more than a single audience in the Reception Hall for Foreign Guests, and the present of a suit of clothes, seeing that he was provided with guards until he left our borders so as not to allow him to beguile the masses. Not to mention that he has been dead for so long–how could [this bone] be allowed to enter the palace?. . . I would beg that this bone be handed over to the authorities, to be thrown into water or fire, to forever destroy its root and base, so that the doubts in the empire are resolved, the beguilement of future generations nipped in the bud. . . .

It can be assumed that his remonstrance exceeded normal limits: after having nearly been executed for his lese majesty, Han Yu was banished to the extreme southeastern part of China; he took fewer risks in his exile in Chaozhou by asking that the crocodiles evacuate the local river under his domain:

> Though weak and feeble, I lower my head to the crocodiles, my heart crushed, trembling in fear, in order to barely manage to survive, thereby dishonoring myself before the people and my subordinates. Moreover, I have received orders from the Son of Heaven to come here and carry out the duties of the prefect. Under these circumstances I cannot but discuss the situation with the crocodiles. If they are endowed with intelligence, may they listen to the warning of the prefect.

The ocean is located to the south of Chaozhou, "the prefecture of the Tides." The vast sea can give life and nourishment to all who return to it, from the largest being like the whale and the rock, to the smallest shrimp or crab. By departing in the morning, the crocodiles would arrive in the evening. Let me make a pact with them: before three days have passed, they must take their horrible mob south to the sea, so as to avoid the officer appointed by the Son of Heaven. If this is not possible in three days, it shall be in five. If it is not possible in five days, they shall be accorded seven. If seven days are not sufficient, it will be clear that they refuse to move and have not accepted the presence of the prefect or listened to his entreaties. Or that the crocodiles are foolish animals, without intelligence, who neither listen to nor understand the words of the prefect. Now, then, whoever scorns the officer appointed by the Son of Heaven, neither obeying him nor moving away to avoid him, as well as the unintelligent beasts, harmful to the people and to other creatures, all these may be put to death. . . .

This petition that accompanied the offerings to the crocodiles is to be read with tongue in cheek, as Han Yu has revealed elsewhere, including his satirical biography of a certain Mao Ying 毛穎, "Tip of the Brush," in which he compares the emperor's casting away a worn-out brush that served him long and loyally to the abandonment of a loyal official who grows old and begins to lose his hair. In the piece that follows, Han allows us to savor the ironic ambiguity of an allegory also aimed at the sovereign and his scholars:

The dragon exhales a sigh which turns into clouds, clouds which assuredly are no more efficacious than the dragon. But the dragon mounts this exhalation, which exhausts the immensity of the celestial mystery, which veils the sun and the moon, glistening between the darkness and the light; he emits lightning and thunder, and through divine transformations causes water to fall on the earth, drenching hills and valleys. Could it be that the clouds themselves are also efficacious?

The clouds are that which the dragon is able to make efficacious. As for the efficacity of the dragon, it is not that which the clouds have made. Nevertheless, if the dragon were not able to reach the clouds, he would have no means to deploy his divine power. He would certainly not know what to do without this support. Strange! For this support is his own emanation. As the Classic of Changes says, "The clouds follow the dragon;" that is to say, "The dragon is that which follows the clouds."

The epitaph and the funeral inscription that Han Yu composed for Liu Zongyuan 柳宗元 (773–819), the other influential ancient-style prose advocate of the Tang dynasty (618–907), have had enduring fame. Han Yu and Liu Zongyuan head the list of "eight great prose writers of the Tang and Song dynasties" and form a pair that critics have enjoyed juxtaposing and comparing. Holding to a much less militant brand of Confucianism, Liu Zongyuan was as open to Taoist and Buddhist ideas as he was to those of Legalism. In disgrace after the abdication of Emperor Shunzong (r. 805), whom he had strongly supported, Liu Zongyuan was exiled almost continually to minor posts in the far south. Ironically, some were sinecures that allowed him the time to foster his literary career. His best-known works come from this period. The anti-Confucian, pro-Legalist campaign of the last phase of the Great Cultural Revolution (1966–1976) valued him highly, giving him star billing and particularly praising his discourse on the feudal regime, *Fengjian lun* 封建論 (On Feudalism). This discourse supports an evolutionary thesis inspired by a rather unorthodox Confucianism. Necessity pushes humans to organize themselves into societies for survival and self-protection, but it is not in response to human will that society is carried toward a confederacy of chiefdoms and finally devoted to a supreme authority in the person of the Son of Heaven (or emperor). The prefectural system is superior to the feudal society that it eliminated. The crises of those governments that employed the prefectural system were caused not by the system, but by other factors. Confucius did not choose the feudal system, he merely survived it. Liu concludes:

Now, the Way of the governing throughout the world generates either order or chaos among the people. Only after causing those who are worthy to occupy the positions above, and those who are unworthy those below, can you achieve order and peace. Now, the feudal regime achieves order through the hereditary succession of positions. To achieve order through hereditary succession, do not those above indeed have to be worthy and those below indeed unworthy? Yet how order and chaos are generated in men is something that cannot be understood. If one desires to profit the altars of a state, one must unify that which the people of that state see and hear; if there are furthermore hereditary nobles living from the emoluments of hereditary fiefs, the grantable fiefs will be exhausted. When sages and worthies are born in this time, there is indeed nowhere to establish them [with fiefs]–this is the result of the feudal system. How could it be that what the Sage [Confucius] determined for governing was reached in this? I would claim, "The feudal system was not the Sage's concept, it was his situation."

It is in his fables, his descriptions of excursions, that Liu Zongyuan appears more captivating than the severe Han Yu; for example, the distressing story of the fawn of Linjiang:

In the course of a hunt, a native of Linjiang [in modern Jiangxi] captured a fawn which he decided to raise. As they entered through his gate, a pack of dogs approached, salivating and wagging their tails. The man was angry and rebuffed them. Thenceforth he would carry the deer to the dogs, so they would get used to his showing it to them, while he forbade them to move. Gradually, he let them play with it. After a time, the dogs all did what the man wanted. As the fawn slowly grew up, it forgot it was a deer and believed the dogs were its good friends. It would butt heads with them and lie down with them, becoming increasingly intimate. The dogs feared their master and were docile and friendly to it. But from time to time they would lick their chops.

After three years, the deer went outside the gate. Seeing a large pack of dogs along the road, it ran to play with them. When they saw it, these other dogs went into a frenzy, joining together to kill and devour it, strewing the remains along the road. The fawn went to its death without being enlightened.

The statesman Ouyang Xiu 歐陽修 (1007–1072), the third of the "eight prose masters," was also the person who "rediscovered" Han Yu's writing, which had been eclipsed by a revival of the parallel-prose style (especially at court) in the late ninth and tenth centuries. Ouyang's "discourses" are among the most appreciated of his prose works, especially those in which he justified the formation of political factions (through which the good could drive away the bad) and that on the eunuchs, which appeared in the dynastic *New History of the Five Dynasties* that he edited, revealing the difficult position of the scholars:

That eunuchs have brought chaos to states since ancient times has its origins deep in the misfortunes caused by women. Women are no more than sexual objects. The noxiousness of the eunuchs, however, does not arise from a single cause. It may be that in being employed in official positions they are close to the sovereign and become familiar with him or that in their thinking they are single-minded and patient. They are able to win favor because of a small talent, to secure affection because of a small act of faith. They wait until they are completely trusted and maintain this trust by frightening the ruler with omens. Although the ruler has loyal ministers and eminent scholars arrayed in his court, he finds them too distant and prefers to rely on those intimates with whom he spends his daily life and takes his meals, those who are before and behind him, to his left and his right. For this reason, those who are before and behind him, to his left and his right, daily become more familiar, the loyal ministers and eminent scholars daily become more estranged, and the ruler's position daily becomes more isolated.

Examiner-in-chief for the "doctoral examinations" of 1057, Ouyang Xiu promoted three of the other "eight great prose writers:" his friend Zeng Gong 曾鞏 (1019–1063), whose "severe style" has not served him well in the opinion of posterity; Su Shi 蘇軾 (1037–1101); and Su's younger brother Su Che 蘇轍 (1039–1112). Numbers seven and eight on the list are the father of the precocious geniuses, Su Xun 蘇洵 (1009–1055), and the politician Wang Anshi 王安石 (1021–1086), most famous for his radical reforms and related prose writings, which, because of their topicality, are of little interest to the modern reader. It is clear, however, that on the literary stage, Su Shi eclipsed them all, including his patron Ouyang Xiu. The question is how to evaluate Su's vast and varied collected works, in which superb poetry vies with his prose writings. The shackles of a rigid Confucianism were cheerily ignored by a spirit enamored with moral and intellectual freedom. This can be seen in the following passage from the dissertation entitled "Xing shang zhong hou zhi zhi lun" 刑賞忠厚之 至論 (On the Penalties and Rewards of Perfecting Loyalty and Generosity), which distinguished the examination papers of Su Shi, scarcely twenty years old, in the view of his "master" Ouyang Xiu. The passage, about a sage ancient ruler contains what seemed a certain allusion to one of the classics. This greatly intrigued the examiners, because they did not recognize the allusion, but they would not admit to the gap in their memories. After allowing Su Shi to pass high on the list of graduates, they questioned the laureate about his source, and Su Shi acknowledged that the anecdote about the largesse of the sage king Yao 堯 was his own invention!

.As the commentary says, "When there is doubt about giving rewards, they should be given widely to demonstrate the royal grace; when there is doubt about giving penalties, they should be widely avoided, to demonstrate the care with which punishments are applied."

In Emperor Yao's time, Gao Yao was the Minister of Justice. He was going to kill a man. Gao Yao said, "Kill him" three times. Yao said,

"Pardon him" three times. For this reason the people of the world feared the firmness with which Gao Yao enforced the law and delighted in the leniency with which Yao applied punishments.

Su Shi might also be considered the precursor of a genre in which the original character of Chinese civilization at its best was depicted–the *xiaopin wen* 小品文 or "essay on minor subjects"–as the opening passage from his "Chaoran Tai ji" 超然臺記 (Notes on the Terrace of Transcendence) illustrates:

> All things merit observation, and since they merit it they are all sources of potential joy. It is not necessary that they be rare or marvelous, beautiful or imposing. A simple beverage of fermented rice is enough to make one feel good; fruits and vegetables can satisfy the appetite. To follow this line of reasoning, where could I go that I would not be happy?

III. The Golden Age of Trivial Literature

Scorned by the ancients as well as the moderns, the free essays in the *xiaopin wen* form enjoyed their greatest popularity during the sixteenth and seventeenth centuries. The genre could nevertheless claim a respectable ancestry, having commenced with a narrative about Confucius which closes chapter 11 of the *Analects*:

> Zilu, Zeng Xi, Ran You, and Gongxi Hua were seated in attendance on Confucius. The Master said, "Forget for a moment that I am your elder. You say among yourselves, 'No one appreciates my talents.' If you did find someone to appreciate them, what would you wish to do?"[3]

---

[3]The implied subject of "appreciating talents" would be the lord of a state

Zilu quickly responded: "Give me a country of one thousand chariots situated between two great countries, ravaged by famine under the pressure of enemy troops. If I were in charge, within three years I would give its people courage and put them back on their feet."

The Master sighed and said, "Ran You, what about you?"

Ran You replied, "Give me a state of twenty to thirty miles square, or even fifteen to twenty miles square. If I were in charge, within three years the people would be well off. As for rites and music, however, that would have to await a gentleman."

"And you, Gongxi Hua?"

"I cannot say that I already have the ability [to rule], but I am ready to learn. In carrying out the affairs of worship in the ancestral temple or in diplomatic gatherings, I am ready to serve as a minor assistant."

"Zeng Xi, what about you?"

A final note died from his lute, then Zeng Xi put the lute aside, stood up [in respect], and replied, "My choice differs from those of the other three."

The Master said, "What harm is there in that? After all, each is expressing his own ambition."

"At the end of spring, in the clothes appropriate to that season, I would like to go to bathe in the river accompanied by five or six men and six or seven youths, to enjoy the breeze, and to return home singing."

The Master heaved a sigh of approval: "I am with you."

The spirit of *xiaopin wen* existed long before the term was applied to the literary mode that prevailed among scholars at the end of the sixteenth century. Witness the *Zazuan* 雜纂 (Miscellanies), attributed incorrectly to the poet Li Shangyin 李商隱 (ca. 813–858), a work which toward the year 1000 perhaps inspired the celebrated *Pillowbook* of the Japanese authoress Sei Shônagon 清少納言, as the following examples from the *Miscellanies* suggest:

---

who would then employ the man he saw as talented.

I. Incongruities: 1. A poor Persian. 7. A butcher reciting sutras.

VIII. Resemblances: 4. Like a tiger, whenever a magistrate moves, he injures people.

XVII. Annoying things: 1. Cutting with a blunt knife. 4. Building a wall that hides the mountains.

XIX. Spoiling the fun: 3. Spreading a mat on moss. 8. Carrying a torch in the moonlight.

XX: Cannot bear to hear: 2. The filthy talk of the marketplace. 4. A young wife mourning her husband.

XXIV: (The Power of) Suggestion: 1. Wearing green gauze in winter makes one feel cold. 4. Heavy curtains suggest someone lurking.

XXX: Contemporary crazes: 6. Adults flying kites. 8. Women cursing in public.

XXXIII: Unlucky: 1. To eat lying down. 5. To write bareheaded.

XXXIX: Lapses: 2. Scolding another's servants. 9. Raising chopsticks before the host asks people to start eating.

The return of ancient-style prose in the eleventh century was a straightforward demand for liberty and spontaneity; it emerged "as water surges forth," in the words of Su Shi. Technique (*fa* 法) was servant to inspiration (*yi* 意). Was this a result of the trauma of the Jurchen and then Mongol incursions from the eleventh through the thirteenth centuries? Under the Mongols (Yuan dynasty, 1279–1368), the entire country was for the first time entirely under the rule of alien conquerors.

After the restoration of Chinese rule in the Ming dynasty (1368–1644), the new capital at Beijing again became the focus of power under the reign of the Yongle emperor (1403–1424). But it was not the center of culture or intellectual activity, which was increasingly found in the Lower Yangtze Valley, around the traditional centers of Nanjing, Suzhou, and Hangzhou. Cliques formed among these intellectuals, polarized by the question of whether to imitate the ancients. Adherents of the type of straightforward prose that Han Yu and Liu Zongyuan advocated now revived the earlier arguments. They advocated seeking inspiration among the ancients, but opposed imitation of any kind. This statement by Yuan Zongdao's 袁宗道 (1560–1600) is typical:

> This is why Confucius said of prose that it sufficed if it made itself understood. Intelligibility is the measure of quality literature. . . . As our contemporaries do not immediately fathom the ancient works that they read, they find "ancient prose" of a marvelous profundity and proscribe the simplicity of modern writers. The ancient and modern prose works were both appropriate to their times and to their language. The rare words and obscure phrases that have aroused the astonished admiration of today's reader–can one know that they were not in their time part of the language of the streets?

The logical response to this argument would have been to adopt the spoken language of each era as the medium of prose. Such pleas had little effect until nearly 1920, however, and the vernacular was then introduced as the medium of elite literature only with great difficulty–it still seemed natural for scholars involved with this linguistic revolution to write their pleas in the classical language.

Yuan Zongdao and his two well-known brothers, Yuan Hongdao 袁宏道 (1568–1610) and Yuan Zhongdao 袁中道 (1570–1624), fell into neglect for several centuries after their works were banned by the Manchus who conquered China and set up the Qing dynasty (1644–1911). In the late Ming, however, Yuan Hongdao was the best-known writer in the family. Yuan Hongdao was originally from Gong'an 公安, in the green and mountainous meridional province of Hubei, and when he was assigned to the capital in an official capacity, he rediscovered the joy of the landscapes surrounding his beloved hometown through literature in his "Wenyi Tang ji" 文漪堂記 (Record of the Hall of Literary Ripples):

> I rented a house where I laid out a small room to the right of the hall to read books in. . . . Above the gate I hung an inscription that read

"The Hall of Literary Ripples."

Someone said: "Here in the capital the noise and the dust hide the sky to the point that it is hazy the whole day long. Yet in this 'hall' there is not anything which could be called a wave or even a pond. Where will you get the ripples to be displayed before you?"

I laughed and said, "It is not a matter of water in the strict sense, not real water. However, there is nothing under heaven which resembles water more than literature. It hurtles down all at once, then suddenly changes course. It returns to heave in dark clouds covering in an instant thousands of miles. . . . I close my gate and arrange my thoughts. My bosom swells and, as if I have bumped into something, I suddenly see a surge of waves, eddies, and ripples rise up like those I saw in former days. And when I take up a book by Sima Qian, Ban Gu, Du Fu, Po Juyi, Han Yu, Ouyang Xiu, Su Xun, or Su Shi, the metamorphoses and wonders of water are all displayed before me. . . . Everything supple and sinuous is water. That is why in my eyes all literature is related to water. Not that I would deny that mountains are as beautiful as literature, but they have a height which cannot be lowered, a rigidity which cannot be made pliable. They are something dead. But water, no. . . ."

Officials were normally transferred to a new post every three years, so scholars were by force of necessity great travelers. It should come as no surprise, therefore, that travel literature was established as early as the second century B.C., in the narratives by Zhang Qian 張騫 about his exploration of countries to the west. Later, Ouyang Xiu kept a journal of his mission to a barbarian court in the eleventh century. But the case of Xu Xiake 徐霞客 (the *hao* of Xu Hongzu 徐宏祖, 1586–1641) seems exceptional: he sacrificed his ambitions for an official career to his passion for long treks in the mountains. His famous journals focus on the object of his observations, but are of a precision that fills modern-day geographers with joy. The following passage is from his "You Wutai Shan riji" 遊五臺山日記 (A Diary of Roaming through the Five Terrace Mountains):

The sixth of the eighth month (31 August 1623): a windstorm arose, but each drop of rain that fell changed into ice. When the wind fell, the sun appeared, like a bead of fire looming suddenly through the jade-blue leaves. When I followed the mountain toward the southwest about a mile, I crossed a ridge and could first see Southern Terrace [one of the Five Terrace Mountains] before me. Ascending further, I found the Lamp Monastery. Along this way the road gradually grew steep. About three miles farther, I climbed the highest peak on the Southern Terrace, where a stupa containing a relic of Mañjusrî stood. Facing north, the other terraces were arrayed in a circle; only to the southeast and the southwest was there a little open space.

This passage gives only a slight indication of the wealth of detail in the diary which vies with even the best modern guides to the Five Terrace Mountains in modern Shanxi.

Chen Jiru 陳繼儒 (1558–1639), a friend of the Xu family who composed a biography for Xu Xiake's father, is perhaps the most representative of the new type of literati who managed to live from what he earned with his writing brush rather than lowering himself to enter an official career. His varied, largely ignored corpus of works includes pithy epigrams such as the following:

A bachelor is as timid as a young virgin. When he begins his official career, he must treat his superiors as a daughter-n-law does her husband's parents. When he retires, like a mother-in-law, he takes pleasure in dispensing advice liberally.

Pardon the offenses of your servants–those in which you are the victim, not those which others have complained about.

It is difficult to truly know others. And those who allow themselves to be known easily are not worth the trouble of getting to know.

After the collapse of the Ming dynasty in 1644, many scholars refused to serve the new masters–the Manchus–because of their loyalty to the fallen regime. Was this the case with Li Yu 李漁 (1611–1680? An admirer of the renowned novelist and dramatist Chen Jiru, Li was also without doubt the most original essayist China has ever produced.

An impenitent hedonist, Li Yu seems to have preferred the independence of a life devoted to pleasure to the servitude of an official life. He gave up his career and resorted to patrons to supplement the income, always insufficient, that he earned from his publications, shamelessly pirated, and also from his theater troupe, to which he contributed his own concubines. It is true that the "poverty" of which he often complains in his correspondence did not prevent him from keeping a household of fifty people. The title that he gave to the successive collections of his works in classical Chinese is significant: *Liweng yijia yan* 笠翁一家言 (Words from the Unique School of Liweng)–Liweng, "the old [fisherman] in a straw hat," was his *zi* or "style." His defense of novelty and a spirit of invention is not without ironic nuances:

> One looks for the old only in people; in things it is only the novel that holds interest. "Novel" is a laudatory qualifier for everything in the world. It is doubly so when it comes to literary art. [As Han Yu wrote:] "How difficult it is to apply oneself to eliminating cliches!" (I, 3).
>
> Recent works sacrifice everything to novelty. They change what can be changed without examining it. But they also trade what should be preserved at all costs to appear innovative. I think the novelty of writing is internal and should not apply to external aspects.

Li Yu's admirable *Xianqing ouji* 閒情偶記 (Occasional Notes Occasioned by Feelings of Idleness) is a seemingly modest compilation that skillfully intertwines some three hundred essays. It is evident from his letters, however, that Li Yu was perfectly aware that the publication of this collection was his crowning achievement. In his claim that he was expressing the self, *xingling* 性靈 (the efficacy of [one's own] nature), the innovative power of the Yuan brothers can certainly be seen. But no one else had the know-how to assume this power so wholeheartedly. Art was supposed to chase away tedium: the expression of the self is the necessary condition, but by itself is not sufficient. A work of art must sustain the interest of others and elicit pleasure. In this Li Yu agreed with Yuan Hongdao on the importance of *qu* 趣, amusement. He took pleasure in employing paradox, with respect to style or situation, and indeed in shocking the reader. As an example, witness the section of his *Xianqing ouji* devoted to the "art of sweeping:"

> A stylish house requires the greatest care in sweeping. But this demands a higher skill than simple servants have. To eliminate dust, it is necessary to begin by splashing water lightly about. This is a method that the ancients have transmitted to us. Not more than one or two people in ten practice it today. The servant boy, naturally lazy, contents himself to sweep—when in fact the one doesn't work without the other.

The poet Yuan Mei 袁枚 (1716–1797) might be called the "Chinese Julia Child" because of his wonderful cookbook entitled *Shidan* 食單 (Menus, 1796), but no one knew better how to communicate the passions of the gourmand than Li Yu; here he relates the art of savoring crabs with an infectious fervor:

> As for the pleasures of the table, I can talk about them all, and my imagination is inexhaustible. But it is only crabs that will not allow me to detail their wonders in full. My spirit savors them with so much delight that I will never forget the taste on my palate until the last day of my life. Why? All my eloquence does not suffice to explain. . . .
> Each year before they appear in the marketplace, I hoard my pennies in expectation. As my family pokes fun at me by saying that I hold crabs more dear than life, I call this money "the vital ransom."

There is no better medicine than a good humor and the pleasures, large and small, that sustain one. Li Yu recounts for us how, during an epidemic in 1630, which had struck his entire family, and him more gravely than the others, the doctor had advised against the consumption of arbutus berries, which he was very fond of:

> I then began to question my family. They set the words of the doctor against me. "A charlatan who knows precious little about it! Go buy them for me with all due speed!" I grumbled. The juice of the berries had scarcely flowed into my mouth when the knot of melancholy that had gripped my breast completely loosened. When what I swallowed reached my stomach, it restored the harmony to my five organs. I fully regained the use of my four limbs. I no longer knew what illness it was I had suffered from. With this spectacle, my family understood that the doctor's warning had proved false, and they allowed me to eat the berries to my heart's content.

To attempt to treat his melancholy by forcing himself to have sexual relations would have been "like compelling a sad person to laugh." But Li Yu admitted that he was incapable of following the good advice of "just exercising more moderation than was his habit" (XVI, 4, 2). On the other hand, there is no better remedy for amorous languor than satisfying thwarted desire:

> Every young boy or young girl, when the desire for love has already begun but they are not yet married, falls ill thereby, not soon to recover. Only this one thing can cure them. Even if the patient is too weak to endure intimate embraces, it suffices to have his beloved come and go before him, to thereby make known to him that [his beloved] already belongs to him. This can relieve most of the lovesickness. It is like someone who obtains a medicine but doesn't take it. Only inhaling its odor still makes him feel better. . . . The filial and charitable sons who care for their parents, the strict fathers as well as the sweet mothers who love their sons, all must prepare this remedy in advance, so as to prevent the illness. (XVI, 6, 3)

When Li Yu speaks of beds in his chapter on furniture, he calls to us with irrefutable eloquence:

> A man lives one hundred years, half of which he passes occupied with the day and the other half occupied with the night. The days he spends in indeterminable places: a hall, a room, a boat, or a carriage. But the nights he knows only to spend in bed. Beds are therefore things in which we have company half the night and which have precedence over our companions. So there is nothing that merits more of our attention.
>
> I am always amazed with my contemporaries who, when looking for a place to live, inquire after a house as if their lives were at stake, but ostensibly neglect the quarters where they would take their rest under the pretext that they are places one does not show to others. But would it then be necessary for our wives, concubines, and servants to go about in rags, with tousled hair and dirty faces, because these human beings, like our beds, are reserved for our view and not that of others? (X, 1, 4)

Of all the pleasures of life, there were few that Li Yu placed above a hot bath, in summer or winter. To the Taoists, who had forbidden such baths in order to "nourish the vital principle," Li Yu replied by likening man to plants, which are believed to give thanks for the rain and the dew (XV, 1, 11). Yet among all of his passions and his aversions, Li Yu confides to us at the end of his work, his maniacal obsession has been the love of writing, a remedy for depression as for anger or a bad mood. Is it not a kind of sickness that causes one to persevere until a literary work is completed?

> What pushes me to this? Most often the hand of the little imp of creation.

It is obvious that Li Yu's defense and illustration of what are viewed by the Confucian tradition as trifling matters, which he manages with so much brilliance, are not as trivial as they may appear. His ideas on literary art provide further demonstration of this situation. They agree with so many Western conceptions that they run the unfair risk of seeming banal to us.

IV. Literary Criticism

Of an inventive mind, Li Yu was a creative craftsman of fiction, according great importance to plot and diction. These emphases were a paradox for Chinese traditional criticism, which usually focused on musical aspects of the opera-theater, a relatively late genre that originated in the twelfth century. For the most part, works devoted to literary criticism were concerned mainly with poetry, specifically the effect of poetry rather than its genesis. The art of literary composition in prose is treated only marginally in the anthologies that gave rise to the revised system of examinations starting in the twelfth century.

With respect to evaluation and classification, the preferred theories were expressed in terse formulae. These tendencies were already apparent in the earliest treatise that has been handed down, that by Cao Pi 曹丕 (187–226), the *Lun wen* 論文 (Discourse on Literature), a fragment preserved in *A Selection of Literature* by Xiao Tong (501–531). Breaking for the first time from the moral and utilitarian point of view, this little work contemplates literature in its aesthetic aspects, for the "*wen* possessed a common trunk that does not differ from its branches," which are the various classical genres, each having its own requirements.

The *Wen fu* 文賦 or "*Fu* on Literature" by Lu Ji 陸機 (261–301) celebrated the mysteries of inspiration, but the most elaborate survey of this dominant current in Chinese literary criticism is the *Wenxin diaolong* 文心雕龍 (The Heart of Literature Carves Dragons) by Liu Xie 劉協 (c. 465–520). The work consists of fifty chapters which treat literary theory and its applications ecumenically, integrating the Confucian tradition with elements of Buddhism. The title of the work conjures up this program–'heart' in the title might also be understood as '[literary] mind'"–artistic works are a product of the spirit of literature. The first chapter treats the "Original *Dao*" or Way:

> Great is the strength of *wen*! . . . When the spirit [the heart] is born,
> the word is established, and through the establishment of the language,
> *wen* [literature] shines forth. It is the Way of a spontaneous nature. . . .

After the first five chapters, which develop the idea that literature is in the nature of things, Liu Xie devotes the nineteen following sections to an examination of literary genres, divided up between those which are *wen* 文 (ornate/belletristic), requiring rhythm and/or rhyme, and those which are *bi* 筆 (brushwork/utilitarian), inclined toward simple clarity of expression. The third part examines, with much finesse, literary composition, literary techniques, and literary sensibilities. The penultimate chapter recaptures the parallel with music in its title, *Zhiyin* 知音 (Understanding Sound); it treats the critical comprehension that must initially take six points of view into consideration:

> 1) Style, 2) Rhetoric, 3) Communicability and flexibility, 4) Rectitude
> and the fantastic, 5) Events and meaning, and 6) Musicality

The fiftieth and final chapter is a postface in which Liu Xie pays homage to his precursors and justifies his enterprise, ending with this distich of praise:

> Literature is indeed a vehicle of the spirit
> And my spirit has been raised in its domicile.

Comparable in importance to the *Wenxin diaolong*, the *Shi pin* 詩品 (Evaluation of Poetry), composed between 513 and 517 by Zhong Rong 鍾嶸, is devoted principally to the pentasyllabic poems of 122 authors of the third to fourth centuries. The most accomplished collected works strike a balance between "description," *fu*, and the *xing-bi*, the stimulating evocation and comparison that transcend the literal sense. The influence of Taoism and Buddhism is even more marked in the *Ershisi shi pin* 二十

四詩品 (Evaluations of Poetry in Twenty-four [Poems]) by Sikong Tu 司
空圖 (837-908).

For Yan Yu 嚴羽, who lived at the turn of the twelfth to the
thirteenth century, the primary role of poetry was to communicate the
knowledge of a transcendental reality beyond words. He borrowed a
good deal of terminology from the Chan sect (Zen, in Sino-Japanese). His
Canglang shihua 滄浪詩話 (Remarks on Poetry by [the Hermit] of the
[River] Canglang) had a decisive influence on the innumerable *shihua*
(remarks on poetry) that followed his. A related genre is the *benshi* 本事
(the facts themselves), works that endeavored to divulge the circumstances
under which poems were produced. All these works, including anthologies,
testify to the preeminence that poetry has always had in the eyes of the
Chinese.

Suggested Further Reading

There is a detailed general survey of Chinese prose in *Indiana Companion,* I: 93–120. The relevant sections of James R. Hightower's *Topics in Chinese Literature* (Cambridge: Harvard University Press, 1950), though somewhat dated, are still useful. David Knechtges's ongoing translation of *Wen xuan or Selections of Refined Literature* (3 vols. to date; Princeton: Princeton University Press, 1982–) is an excellent source on early Chinese prose. A full survey of landscape depiction is presented in Richard E. Strassberg, trans., *Inscribed Landscapes: Travel Writing from Imperial China* (Berkeley: University of California Press, 1994), including selections from most of the writers introduced above. In *Indiana Companion,* see also entries for these writers as well as *"Ku–wen kuan–chih"* 古文觀止 and *"Ku–wen tz'u lei–tsuan"* 古文辭類纂, I: 500–501 and 501–503, respectively.

Narrative Art and Historical Records

Dawson, Raymond. *Historical Records.* Oxford: Oxford University Press, 1994.

Durrant, Stephen. *The Cloudy Mirror: Tension and Conflict in the Writings of Sima Qian.* Albany: State University of New York Press, 1995.

Nienhauser, William H., Jr., ed. Nienhauser et al., trans. *The Grand Scribe's Records* Volume 1: *The Basic Annals of Pre-Han China.* Volume 7: *The Memoirs of Pre-Han China.* Bloomington: Indiana University Press, 1994.

Pohl, Karl–Heinz. *Cheng Pan–ch'iao: Poet, Painter and Calligrapher.* Nettetal: Steyler Verlag, 1990.

Watson, Burton. *Records of the Grand Historian: Han Dynasty I and II.* Revised ed. 2 vols. Hong Kong and New York: Renditions-Columbia University Press, 1993.

___. *Records of the Grand Historian: Qin Dynasty*. Vol. 3. Revised ed. Hong Kong and New York: The Research Centre for Translation, The Chinese University of Hong Kong and Columbia University Press, 1993.

The Return of the "Ancient Style"

Ch'en, Jo-shui. *Liu Tsung-yüan and Intellectual Change in T'ang China, 773–819*. Cambridge: Cambridge University Press, 1992.

Chen, Yu-shih. *Images and Ideas in Chinese Classical Prose: Studies of Four Masters*. Stanford: Stanford University Press, 1988. Studies of Han Yu, Liu Zongyuan, Ouyang Xiu, and Su Shi.

Egan, Ronald C. *The Literary Works of Ou-yang Hsiu (1007–72)*. Cambridge: Cambridge University Press, 1984.

___. *Word, Image and Deed in the Life of Su Shi*. Cambridge: Council on East Asian Studies and the Harvard-Yenching Institute, 1994.

Hartman, Charles. *Han Yü and the T'ang Search for Unity*. Princeton: Princeton University Press, 1985.

"*Ku-wen.*" In *Indiana Companion*, I: 494–500.

Nienhauser, William H., Jr. et al. *Liu Tsung-yüan*. Boston: Twayne, 1973.

The Golden Age of Trival Literature

"Chang Tai" 張岱. In *Indiana Companion*, I: 220–221.

"Li Yü" 李漁. In *Indiana Companion*, I: 557–559.

Literary Criticism

"Literary Criticism." In *Indiana Companion*, I: 49–58.

Liu, James J. Y. *Chinese Theories of Literature*. Chicago: University of Chicago Press, 1974.

Owen, Stephen, trans. *Readings in Chinese Literary Thought*. Cambridge: Harvard University Press, 1992.

Rickett, Adele, ed. *Chinese Approaches to Literature from Confucius to Liang Ch'i-ch'ao*. Princeton: Princeton University Press, 1978.

Wong, Siu–kit, trans. *Early Chinese Literary Criticism.* Hong Kong: Joint
    Publishing, 1983.

.

Chapter 3. Poetry

The preeminence of poetry in the Chinese tradition owes much to a language and writing system that from early times was closely associated with music and painting. The installation of the first imperial regime, the Qin (221–207 B.C.), favored this evolution, since the Qin rulers preferred the carefully constructed formulae and irrefutable citations of verse to the more threatening eloquence of the rhetoricians and their prose. The triumph of ritualism in the succeeding Han dynasty (206 B.C.–220 A.D.) solidified the position of poetry, which had been tied from the beginning to rituals and ceremony.

Long written anonymously as popular or ritual verse, poetry did not begin to become personalized–and professionalized–until the third century A.D.; many of the early personal poems used new forms which had emerged from the fertile ground of popular literature. It was the sixth century before the most characteristic form of Chinese poetry appeared: a rhymed quatrain of heptasyllabic or pentasyllabic lines that took its rhythm from tonal opposition and that adhered to a strict parallelism in the first distich. The ideal was to express the most with the least. Poetic language strove for ambiguity while reducing the number of grammatical words–which the Chinese call "empty words"–to the minimum required for intelligibility. An effect of richness was obtained through implicit images and literary allusions. To this were added the graphic evocations of a writing system autonomous from the language itself. Over the centuries, detailed commentaries have sometimes attempted to impose a word-for-word interpretation, something to which a Chinese poem can rarely be reduced. Would not the critic inspired by Buddhism say that great beauty is inexpressible? Poetic language, laden with tradition, prefers to allude to this beauty rather than speak of it, which lends itself to multiple readings.

The most important verse forms in China, in rough chronological order, have been the ancient *shi* 詩 of the *Shi jing* (twelfth-sixth centuries

B.C.); the *sao* 騷 (laments) of the state of Chu in the third and fourth
centuries B.C. and its successor, the fu 賦 (rhapsody) of the Han dynasty
and after; *yuefu* 樂府 (music bureau) poetry and its continuation, *guti shi*
古體詩 (ancient-style verse), from the Han dynasty to the sixth century
A.D.; *jinti shi* 近體詩 (modern-style verse), including *lü shi* 律詩 (regulated,
eight-line verse) and *jueju* 絕句 (quatrains), which flourished in the Tang
dynasty; the *ci* 詞 (lyric), which began as a quasi-oral genre in the Tang;
and the *qu* 曲 (arias), which developed in conjunction with the opera-theater
and were first popular during the Yuan dynasty (1279–1368).

I. The Two Sources of Ancient Poetry

We have seen above the role that Confucius assigned to the *Classic
of Poetry*, the *Shi jing*. This classic was memorized by all literati and was
essentially the source of a type of poetry designed to "express the intention"
(*yanzhi* 言志) through a poetic text based in nature which offers an implicit
comparison with a human situation. But the *Shi jing* was primarily a
source of inspiration, rather than a model, as so much of its language
quickly became "archaic" and its prosody, viewed from later times, peculiar.

1. The Songs of Chu. The *Chu ci* 楚辭 (Words of the State of
Chu) offer another source of inspiration, that of unbridled and despairing
lyricism. Compiled with commentary by Wang I 王逸 (d. 158 A.D.) in
the second century A.D., the collection consists of seventeen distinct works
written by authors from various eras, works that include nearly one hundred
poems, each composed on one of two distinct prosodic models. These
models involve longer lines (usually with six syllables), with the caesura
or line break punctuated by the archaic exclamation "*xi!*" (pronounced at
that time, it is thought, like "ah!"). The final piece, *Jiu si* 九思 (Nine
Thoughts), is a sort of pastiche by the commentator himself which attributes
the first seven poems to the quasi-legendary figure Qu Yuan 屈原 (ca.
340–278), a loyal minister of the large southern state of Chu who was
rejected by a sovereign incapable of recognizing his merits. His suicide

by drowning is commemorated by the riverine festivals of the summer solstice (the fifth day of the fifth lunar month) in South China. Most of these poems are laments, *sao* 騷, the longest of which is the first, *Li sao* 離 騷 (*Lament for the Separation* [*from the King of Chu*]), the only one of these poems that modern criticism still attributes to Qu Yuan.

The *Li sao* is also regarded as the first poem in Chinese literature to have been intended for a reader (rather than a listener) and to have been based on personal inspiration. The poet expresses himself in the first person in order to launch himself on an ecstatic quest, filled with mythological allusions that are often quite obscure to the modern reader; he moves through the heavens, seeking a divinity that the commentators identify as his sovereign. The texts seem to be imitations of shamanistic declamations, echoes of the culture of the meridional states of South China, whose traditions were lost when Qin unified the empire in the late second century B.C. Here is a passage from the *Li sao*:

> I watered my horse at the Pool of Heaven,
> Tied my reins to the Daybreak Tree,
> Broke off a branch to strike the sun [which rose there],
> And freely I wandered at my ease. (lines 193–196)

The *Nine Songs, Jiu ge* 九歌, which follow the *Li sao*, seem to call for interpretation as dialogues between a medium, a priest or sorcerer, and a divinity. Thus the celebrated *Princess of the River Xiang* (*Xiang furen* 湘婦 人) whom the poet's persona encounters:

> In the morning I drive my horses along the River,
> In the evening I ford the waters toward western cliffs;
> I hear the beautiful one call me to her,
> And together we depart, driving the horses up. . . .

The *Heavenly Questions, Tian wen* 天問 (not "Heaven Questioned" as it is sometimes understood–Heaven, the commentator rightly tells us, is presented as a series of sarcastic riddles attributed to Qu Yuan but with no connection to the tone or the prosodic form of the elegies), refer to ancient myths and legends, as in the following:

> The sun came out of the Valley of Warm Waters, then took his rest at Murky Cliff. How many miles had he [the sun] gone from morning until dusk?

> Kunlun has Hanging Gardens; where are they situated? How many miles high are its nine-fold walls? Who passes through the gates in its four sides?

> Why are the flowers of the Daybreak Tree bright before Xi He, the sun's charioteer, has risen?

> The snake that swallowed an elephant–how big was it?

One comes back to poetry in the *Nine Declarations, Jiu zhang* 九章, of which *The Elegy on the Orange, Ju song* 橘頌, in eighteen lines, is commonly considered a youthful work:

> Among the fine trees of Mother Earth and August Heaven,
> The orange made itself at home here;
> Receiving their orders not to move, it grows in this southern state.
> Its roots deep and firm, hard to transplant, making it more constant.

The fifth piece, *Yuan you* 遠遊 (Distant Journey), in which the persona is again off on a heavenly quest, is thought to be a Taoist-inspired imitation of the *Li sao* of a relatively late date.

The *Nine Arguments, Jiu bian* 九辯, traditionally attributed to Song Yu 宋玉, a direct disciple of Qu Yuan, heralds the style of the *fu* through an exuberant lyricism that defies translation.

The *fu* 賦 (rhapsody or prose-poem), in rhythmic prose and rhymed, was meant to be recited and is difficult to distinguish from the *sao*. Since the *sao* was of southern origins, it is not surprising that the first dated *fu* (174 B.C.), a meditation on the evil auspices of the owl, *Funiao fu* 鵩鳥賦, was also written in that region by Jia Yi 賈誼 (200–168 B.C.). In another *fu*, titled *Diao Qu Yuan* 弔屈原 (*Grieving for Qu Yuan*), Jia Yi made clear his personal identification with Qu Yuan. In the *Seven Exhortations, Qi fa* 七發, by Mei Sheng 枚乘 (d. 141 B.C.), the genre reached new heights by abandoning the mode of complaint seen in works such as *Grieving for Qu Yuan* in favor of a positive lyricism expressed indirectly under cover of what were claimed to be moral admonitions.

2. Poetry of the Han Court. With the unequaled works of Sima Xiangru 司馬相如 (ca. 177–119), *fu* (rhapsodies) became part of the literature and splendor of the second-century Han dynasty imperial court under Emperor Wu 武 (r. 140–87 B.C.), demanding of its audience a frightening amount of erudition. It is understandable that Sima Xiangru's youthful elopement with a rich widow from his home area of Shu touched the popular imagination more than the interminable lyrical flights of the major works he wrote years later at court, *Zixu fu* 子虛賦 (*Rhapsody of the Hunting Parks of the Sovereigns of Qi and of Chu*) and *Shanglin fu* 上林賦 (*Rhapsody of a Hunt in the Party of the Son of Heaven*).

From the celebrated *fu* of Ban Gu 班固 (32–92) on the two capitals of the Han, Luoyang and Chang'an, *Liangdu fu* 兩都賦, through the end of the imperial regime in the early twentieth century, a number of authors distinguished themselves in this difficult genre that depicts the grandeur and history of a location in rhymed prose.

At the other extreme of the spectrum of Chinese poetics are found short poems of a rugged simplicity that could be called "emotional improvisations"; we know a small number of them thanks to Sima Qian's *Records of the Grand Historian,* which recalls most notably the song by the

founder of the Han dynasty, Liu Bang 劉邦 (256–195 B.C.). Liu had
begun life as a peasant, but wrote this when as an old man he stopped by
his home town after becoming emperor of all of China:

> A great wind arises, the clouds fly up!
> My majesty increases within the seas as I return to my old village.
> How will I obtain fierce warriors to guard the four directions?

Simple language, often directly accessible to the modern reader,
characterizes the most elaborate of the poems closely related to these
"improvisations," the *yuefu* 樂府 or "music bureau" poems. Said to be
compositions of the "Music Bureau," which was founded in 177 B.C. to
collect folk songs and present them at court as a means to convey the
mood and desires of the citizenry, more than five hundred of these
poems exist today. Scholars soon applied themselves to composing poems
with the same titles and in the same style on a huge range of themes,
from war to love. These poems, known as "literary *yuefu*," were handed
down along with the original folk songs through anthologies compiled
many centuries later (the major collection dates from the twelfth century
A.D.). They often pose irresolvable problems of dating, attribution, and
interpretation, since the most ancient texts and those which are the most
authentically "popular" do not seem to be homogenous, but were created
rather by combining several songs with the same theme and title.

Such is not the case for the famous ancient-style poem on a fan
titled "A Song of Remorse" (*Yuan ge xing* 怨歌行) attributed to Lady Ban
班, the great-aunt of the historian and favorite of Emperor Cheng 成 (r.
33–7 B.C.), who soon (in 16 B.C.) was supplanted in the emperor's eyes
by the singer Zhao, popularly called "Flying Swallow:"

> A newly torn strip of fine white silk
> As unsullied as frost and snow.
> Cut into a "shared-pleasure" fan,

Carefully rounded like the full moon.
No matter where the lord goes, tucked into his sleeve,
When moved, it stirs him a light breeze.
Often feared, the arrival of the autumn season
The cool winds that carry off the fiery heat,
Causing it to be tossed into the bamboo hamper–
Favor and love cut off before they run their course.

The shared-pleasure fan was made of two silk faces sewn together,
combining Chinese characters that suggested a happy union, a relationship
which the perfect roundness of the fan suggests will be unending. Aside
from the poetic depiction of the fan, however, the poem offers several
subtexts. The first is an implicit comparison of Lady Ban to the fan. As
she approaches the autumn of her years, she too has been cast off by the
emperor. But the first six lines are also reminiscent of Flying Swallow, the
"newly torn strip of fine white silk" who is now "tucked into the emperor's
sleeve." This poem in pentasyllabic verse was possibly written by a scholar.
The *yuefu*, on the other hand, preferred tetrasyllables or irregular lines, as
in the following song, "West Gate" (*Hsi men xing* 西門行), composed in an
epicurean tone:

Passing the gate to the West,
With each step I think of him.
If we don't take our pleasure today,
What are we waiting for?
Take your pleasure!
Take your pleasure when the proper time arrives!
Why sit suffering anxious thoughts?
Should we again wait for "next time?"
Brew fine wine!
Grill fatty beef!
Shout out that which your heart desires–
Why try to resolve worrisome concerns!. . .

Although the twenty-four lines of this poem (only the first half is presented above) vary from three to seven syllables, the following poem, the last of the "Nineteen Ancient Poems" (*Gu shi shijiu shou*, 古詩十九首), returns to a regular pentasyllabic rhythm. This famous series of anonymous poems is probably a remnant of a type of verse written during the first and second centuries A.D.:

> The full moon, how clear,
> Shining on my gauze bed-curtains.
> Troubled, sorrowful–I cannot sleep;
> I take up my robe, rise to pace.
> Though they say traveling is a joy,
> There's nothing better than coming home early!
> Outside I walk about anxiously–
> Whom should I tell of my sorrowful longing?
> I crane my neck, then return to my chamber
> As tears fall, soaking my clothes.

Following the example of the "airs of the states" in the *Classic of Poetry*, these popular songs, adopted for use at court and reworked by scholars, would become a genre favored by poets, including the best-known Chinese bards. The early literati *yuefu* were merely imitations of the originals, but during the eighth and ninth centuries, some of the major Tang poets used the form in combination with themes critical of contemporary society to create a new genre: "new *yuefu*" (*xin yuefu* 新樂府). These new *yuefu* also appealed to the literati, because they allowed them to escape the rigid prosodic rules of the prevailing poetic genres.

Before we leave the early *yuefu*, however, it is important to acknowledge the role of erotic themes in *yuefu* written in the South, themes that expanded rapidly into a mode of writing at the courts of the southern regimes between the fourth and sixth centuries A.D.

3. Erotic Poetry. Under the veil of modesty, which allowed sexually suggestive poems to be read as political allegories, eroticism is absent from the high literature of the Chinese. Because of Confucian propriety and bigotry, scholars could not commit themselves openly to the erotic. It was not without difficulty that the French businessman, diplomat, and sometimes author, George Soulié de Morant (1878–1955) managed around 1920 to get his hands on an anthology by Lei Jin published in 1914, *Wubaijia xiangyan shi* 五百家香豔詩, *Poems of Perfumed Lascivity by Five hundred Authors (Anthologie de l'amour chinois. Poèmes de lascivité parfumée.)*, not less than 2,318 works from more than 400 poets of the seventeenth century or earlier. What we have been able to learn of the ancient folk literature, however, indicates that singers and authors of common origin ignored these restrictions against the portrayal of the erotic. In the poems and songs of these free spirits there is no lack of the erotic, which they admired as natural and spontaneous. It is often explained that with the eclipse of Confucianism and the swing to Taoism between the third and sixth centuries, eroticism was afforded a place in high literature as part of the "court style" (*gongti* 宮體), a place it never relinquished. Whatever the case, the *Yutai xinyong* 玉臺新詠 (*New Songs from the Jade Terrace*) is the classic anthology of these poems. Compiled around 545 by Xu Ling 徐陵 (507–583), it consists of 656 poems, some by approximately 100 poets from as early as the third century B.C., but many simply anonymous "ancient poems" or *yuefu*. Among the best of these is the dramatic "Mulberry Tree along the Path" (*Mo shang sang* 陌上桑). This narrative poem tells of Luofu 羅敷, a young woman "more than fifteen, but less than twenty," who is picking mulberry leaves to feed to silkworms–a typical female task. Surprised by an imperial envoy on horseback while at work, she repulses his advances by reminding him that he has a wife and she a husband. Some commentators believe the amorous envoy was none other than her husband, Qiu Hu 秋胡, who had been away on official duty and did not recognize his own wife.

The poetess known as Ziye 子夜 ("Midnight," d. 386) seems much less inclined to resist any advances, as the following poems from her legacy–all titled "Midnight"–illustrate:

> Holding my skirt about me, the sash untied
> I paint my brows and come to the front window.
> My gauze skirts are easily blown around;
> If they open a little, blame the spring breeze.

Women were to remain in the back rooms of the house. Thus the erotic image of a woman seductively dressed is enhanced by her daring to come to a front window. The spring breeze and her gauze skirts also figure in the next poem:

> In the spring grove, blossoms so seductive,
> For the spring birds, thoughts so sad.
> The spring breeze redoubles desire
> As it blows open my gauze skirts.

The final example is a steamy account of love fulfilled:

> For many nights I've not put up my hair,
> Silky strands drape across my shoulders.
> As I wind myself around my lover's lap,
> What place is there on him I cannot love?

II. The Golden Age of Chinese Poetry

The important place accorded erotic themes revealed the new attitudes toward life that were beginning to develop as early as the chaotic last years of the Han dynasty (202 B.C.-A.D. 220). The Jian'an 建安 era (196–220) heralded the birth of a poetry that sought to reveal personal emotions rather than–as with the *Shi jing*–to "express the intentions." According to the formula devised by Lu Ji 陸機 (261–303) in his *Wen fu*

文賦 (Rhapsody on Literature), "poetry consisted of patterns of verbal splendor which were founded in sentiment."

1. From Aesthetic Emotion to Metaphysical Flights. Cao Zhi 曹植 (192–232), the estranged younger brother of the reigning emperor of the new Wei dynasty, Cao Pi 曹丕 (187–266), was the most gifted member of a family that was equally distinguished in warfare and literature. When Cao Pi attempted to fluster his younger brother by ordering him to compose some lines of verse as he was walking, Cao Zhi shamed his elder by coming up with his "Poem Written within Seven Steps" (*Qibu shi* 七步詩). Whether or not the story behind the poem is authentic, this little allegory should have perplexed and embarrassed his suspicious brother:

> Boiling beans over burning bean–stalks
> The strained salty juice will do for a sauce.
> Bean-stalks beneath the pot burning,
> Beans in the pot weeping.
> Originally both sprang from the same root,
> So what is the great urgency to simmer us?!

The Caos served as patrons for the pleiad of literary men of the Jian'an era, of which the best-known poet is probably Wang Can 王粲 (177–217). His evocations of the miseries of the times, compiled in a series entitled "Qi ai shi" 七哀詩 (Seven Lamentations), are poignant; the third stanza of the first poem reads thus:

> Along the road there is a woman starving,
> Who abandons the child in her arms among the grasses.
> She turns back hearing its tearful cries,
> But wipes her tears and moves on alone. . . .

"Eighteen Stanzas on the Barbarian Reed–Whistle" (*Hu jia shiba pai* 胡笳十八拍), written in a style similar to the *Chu ci* and attributed to Cai Yan 蔡琰 (b. ca. 178), the daughter of the noted poet Cai Yong 蔡邕 (133–192), tells of her eighteen-year exile among the Xiongnu barbarians, from which she returned in about 192; her complaint had a strong influence on subsequent writings on themes related to banishment.

In the following generation, because of their penchant for escaping from society through mysticism and drink, the major poets were grouped together by later scholars under the rubric "The Seven Sages of the Bamboo Grove" *(Zhulin qi zi* 竹林七子). Ruan Ji 阮籍(210–263) and Xi Kang 嵇康 (223–262), the most celebrated of the group, left some hermetic works and Ruan's very difficult "Songs of What Is in My Heart" *(Yonghuai shi* 詠懷詩), a series of eighty-two poems. Here, for example, is number fourteen, which depicts the poet languishing through the night:

> To open autumn the cool breezes begin,
> The crickets cry through the bed curtains.
> Things of nature move me to great sorrow–
> Grief so strong it causes the heart to mourn.
> I have much to say, but whom can I tell?
> Many words, but no one to whom to lay forth my plaint.
> A slight breeze blows my silken sleeves,
> The bright moon shines with a clear brilliance.
> The cock at dawn cries in the tall tree,
> I order my carriage to turn around and go back.

Next was Tao Yuanming 陶淵明 (later *ming* Qian 潛, 365–427), highly admired by the poets of the Golden Age because he demonstrated that one could write more profound verse using simple words. From an old family that had fallen into obscurity, he embodied the idea of the middle class of literati, who both sought and were repulsed by the idea of an official career. His hedonism accented with stoicism led him to sing of wine and the country life. It seems that his dialogue of "body, shadow and soul" in three poems, *Xing ying shen, san shou*形影身三首, was influenced by Buddhism; the word which is translated here as "body" is literally "form" and seems to render the Sanskrit *rûpa,* which designates the illusionary reality of the senses. To the "body's" argument that it is better to benefit from each day as it passes rather than to search for an impossible immortality, the shadow opposes nobler aspirations, a Confucian reply to a Taoist point of view. The soul calms their quarrel through the aloofness of wisdom:

> Although we are different entities,
> In life we are dependent on each other.
> Bound to share the same good and evil–
> How could I refrain from speaking to you on this?
> The Three Emperors of old, the Great Sages,
> Where are they now?
> Peng Zu loved his long life,
> But even he wanted to stay when he had to go.
> In old age or youth, death is the same,
> For the wise or the stupid, there's really no difference.
> By drinking daily you might be able to forget,
> But won't that shorten your allotted years?
> To do good always brings pleasure,
> But there's often no one to praise you for it.
> To dwell on this will harm my life–
> Just follow fate as you go ahead,
> Ride the waves of the Great Change,
> Not happy, but also not afraid.
> When it is time to go, then you must go–
> No need to be overly concerned.

What Chinese hasn't heard of Tao's *Record of Peach Blossom Fount (Taohua yuan ji* 桃花源記*),* a tale of the goodness and purity of a lost village nestled in a ring of mountains that had escaped time and the agents of the state? The village was discovered by a fisherman who had lost his way. After spending some time in this idyllic valley, he returned to his home, never again to find the entryway. Tao Qian often celebrated the "spirits" these immortals brewed from fermented cereals. Indeed, wine was a major part of the culture of the Period of Disunion, both as a means to escape the pressures of service to the state and as a method of transcendence. Nevertheless, Tao pondered putting an end to his drinking in a poem entitled "On Stopping Wine" *(Zhi jiu* 止酒), in which he cleverly includes the word "stop" in each of the twenty pentasyllabic lines. It ends thus:

> Day after day I was on the point of stopping it–
> but my pulse stopped beating regularly;
> I only knew there was no pleasure in stopping,
> I didn't yet know stopping could benefit me!
> Gradually I realized that stopping would do me good.
> This morning I actually did stop.
> Through this single stop,
> I will stop atop the immortal cliffs of Fusang.
> Will my bright face stop on this old visage?
> How can it stop for a myriad years?

The point is that immortality without pleasure is perhaps not what Tao was seeking.

Finally, Tao sang of the pleasures of the return from officialdom to country life in his "Guiqu lai xi ci" 歸去來兮辭 (Rhapsody on Returning, Going Back), written in 405:

> Return, go back!
> Though fields and gardens are filled with weeds–why not go back?
> It was I who made my mind servant to the body.
> Why should I be devastated and sorrow alone!

Suddenly I see that what has passed cannot be remedied,
But understand that the future can be pursued.
Actually I haven't gone that far along the wrong way,
And am aware that today's rights can put aside yesterday's wrongs.

In contrast to Tao is the great poet of the mountains and tormented
nature, Xie Lingyun 謝靈運 (385–443). Xie was an aristocrat whose verse
pleaded for enlightenment and sudden illumination. He died stoically as
a confirmed Buddhist, condemned for his part in a rebellion against the
government. Only about one hundred poems remain from what was
once a much larger corpus, all known for their difficult diction; here are
the opening lines from his "Spending the Night on the Cliff over Stone
Gate" *(Shimen yanshan su* 石門岩上宿):

In the morning I pick orchids from the park,
Fearing that they will wither in the frost;
In the evening I return to sleep at the edge of the clouds,
Where I sport with the moon upon these rocks.
The singing of the birds tells me they are settling for the night,
As leaves drop from trees, I know the wind has risen. . . .
The pseudonym Hanshan 寒山 (Cold Mountain) perhaps hid a
group of poets inspired by Chan Buddhism who were active during the
sixth century. The following is one of their typical untitled poems:

My heart resembles the autumn moon:
A pool of jade green, clear, bright, and pure.
What other object would sustain this metaphor–
Tell me, what should I say?

At the other end of the spectrum of sixth-century verse, Shen Yue 沈約
(441–553), a courtier, was working on a system of tonal rules for poetic
composition which eventually led to a greater role for form in verse as
well as the greatest poems of the Tang dynasty (618–907).

2. The Age of Maturity. The complete collection of Tang dynasty (618–907) poetry, which was published in 1707 at the order of the emperor Kangxi, contained nearly 50,000 poems by some 2,200 different authors who lived almost a thousand years ago. The Tang remains almost unrivaled in both the quantity and the quality of poetic production. This production was enhanced because the most highly esteemed of the various examinations leading to official careers was the poetry exam; oddly enough, this was an examination that some of the most illustrious poets failed. But the Tang was also a privileged moment in which the literary culture, poised between tradition and creation, attained a certain maturity, in particular the eighth-century or "high Tang," which was seen as the apogee. It was preceded by "early Tang" verse of the seventh century and followed by the "middle and late Tang" poets of the ninth.

Meng Haoran 孟浩然 (689–740) was the first major name to emerge from the intense poetic activity concentrated around the court in the seventh century. Shortly after his ascension, however, three of the greatest poets that China has ever produced came on the literary scene: Wang Wei 王維 (701–761), Li Bai 李白 (701–762), and Du Fu 杜甫 (712–770).

Like Wang Wei, with whom he associated, Meng Haoran was a protégé of a statesman, Zhang Jiuling 張九鈴 (678–740), himself a distinguished poet. The personality of Meng Haoran has been somewhat eclipsed by his friend Wang Wei, but the following poem, "Spring Dawn" *(Chun xiao* 春曉), made famous through its selection by anthologists and translators alike, demonstrates Meng's poetic talent:

> Spring slumber won't awake to dawn,
> Everywhere I hear the sound of birds calling.
> During the night, sounds of wind and rain–
> I wonder how many flower petals have been falling?

Wang Wei was both painter and poet. His landscape paintings are said to have included poetry and his verses to be filled with lovely scenes. In his time, he was better known as an artist. But none of his paintings remain, whereas more than four hundred poems have survived. "Red Peony" *(Hong Mutan* 紅牡丹), though not one of his best known, suggests the delicate and artistic touch of his brush:

> A voluptuous green, but calm and sedate;
> Dressed in a faded red which deepens in places.
> The blossom's about to break apart, its heart crushed–
> How could it understand the beauties of springtime?

Li Bai and Du Fu form a pair at once complementary and opposed–the first a fantastic genius, tempted by esoteric Taoism, who allowed himself to follow spontaneity and inspiration; the second classical and practical, animated by a Confucian concern for society and tormented by the problems of his personal relationships.

Li Bai's origins remain a subject of controversy. The preferred account is that he was ethnically a Han Chinese, descended from a clan that had been exiled to Central Asia. Despite the legends which surround Li Bai's personality like a halo–a much different case from that of Du Fu–he was actually a connoisseur of barbarian writings, texts that were inaccessible to the jealous buffoons at the Chinese court. In fact, the poet was frequently in the company of Emperor Xuanzong (r. 712–756) between 742 and 744. Soon after, however, he was expelled from court, probably at the instigation of his envious colleagues, and dismissed from his position as archivist. From that time on he was almost constantly on the move, until a few years after the onset of the catastrophic rebellion of An Lushan in 755, when he was imprisoned for a time, wrongly accused of treason. More than one thousand poems in a great variety of forms and styles are attributed to him. Li Bai invented some of the forms himself (or perhaps borrowed them from foreign sources). Although he had met most of the great poets of the times, he was best understood by his junior colleague Du Fu, who clearly recognized his genius; Li's reputation, however, did not begin to shine until the following generation, thanks in particular to the then immensely popular poet Bai Juyi 白居易 (772–846), who showed such admiration for Li Bai's verse.

Li Bai composed perhaps the most popular poem in Chinese literature–at the very least, the most popular among the overseas Chinese–"Jingye si" 靜夜思 (Thoughts on a Quiet Evening):

> Before the bed, how clear the bright moonlight,
> As if it were frost covering the ground.
> I raise my eyes toward the moon which gleams,
> Then lower my head, midst thoughts of my native place.

This pentasyllabic quatrain does not contain a single word which is not in common usage today. The same simplicity is found in the most celebrated of Li Bai's four ancient-style poems, titled "Yuexia du zhuo" 月下獨酌 (Drinking Alone under the Moon). It is important to note that in China past–as well as China present–drinking was usually a festive group activity, each member of the party expected to toast and encourage the others:

> A jug of wine, midst the flowers–
> With no close friend I pour my own wine;
> Raising my cup, I toast the bright moon,
> Facing my shadow, we make a threesome.
> The moon doesn't understand how to drink,
> My shadow vainly follows me along.
> To be companions for a while,
> We take our pleasure to celebrate spring.
> As I sing, the moon prances about,
> As I dance, my shadow becomes lost.
> When sober, we share each other's joy,
> Once drunk, each goes his own way.
> Forever bound to emotionless entertainment,
> Let us arrange to meet in the Milky Way.

The misery of the warfare that followed the Rebellion of An Lushan, in which Li Bai became involved, left only a few echoes in his works. His famous poem in irregular verse on the "Hard Road to Shu" *(Shu dao nan* 蜀道難) or modern Sichuan province, where the former emperor fled and took refuge some years later, was wrongly interpreted as an allusion to these events. Here Li Bai depicts the rigors of passage:

> . . . at the highest point, the six dragon-like steeds reach the place where
>   the sun returns;
> At the lowest, the twisting river breaks back in crashing waves.
> At heights that the immortal crane cannot fly across,
> The gibbons anguish as they pull themselves up!
> How many hairpin turns of black mud?
> In a hundred steps, nine bends wind the rock face.
> One feels Orion in passing The Well, the eyes raise, the breath short,
> And sits down with a deep sigh, hands rubbing panting chests.

Du Fu 杜甫 (712–770) met the elder poet Li Bai toward 745. Almost immediately Du pledged to Li admiration without limits, which was made famous in several of Du's poems. Perhaps the best known of those is the first of two poems titled "Dreaming of Li Bai" *(Meng Li Bai* 夢 李白), written about 758; Du Fu expresses in these sixteen five-syllable lines his anxiety for Li Bai, then condemned to exile, and imagines that the soul of the elder poet comes to visit him:

> Since you may have died and left me, I've already swallowed my tears;
> If we're separated in life, the anguish is constant.
> From South of the Jiang in the pestilential territories,
> There is no news of the banished one.
> My old friend has entered my dreams,
> Clearly I have long been thinking of him.
> Now that you are held by a prisoner's bonds,
> What use is it that you have wings?

I fear that this is not the soul of a living being–
The road is so long it cannot be known.
As the soul arrived, the maple grove was green,
When the soul went back, the pass was black.
The setting moon spreads its light across the rafters of the room,
Seeming almost to illuminate your face.
The waters are deep and the waves broad,
They will not let you be caught by a kraken!

Nearly 1,500 poems by Du Fu have come down to us, representing only a small portion of an œuvre which must have been much larger. During the eleventh century he became the prince of Chinese poetry, yet he does not figure in any anthology prior to the tenth century, having failed the civil service examinations and enjoyed only a brief and obscure career at court. His biographies distinguish three periods in his life: his youth (731–745), the sojourn in the capital (746–756), and then the exile and his many travels through the South until his death in 770. The last period is the richest. One finds in it many more evocations of his youth than of the period he spent in Chang'an. It seems Du Fu gradually developed an interest more retrospective than prospective.

One of the earliest works by Du Fu to become famous was his "Ballad of the Army Carts" *(Bingju xing* 兵車行), written in 750, a few years before the empire sank into the miseries of the war that followed the rebellion, which began in 755. This poem of irregular length–twenty-five lines–depicts the sufferings of the conscripts required to combat the menace of the emerging power of the Tibetans in the Sichuan region. This is accomplished in a speech the poet imagines one of these soldiers making:

The carts creak and grind, the horses whinny and blow,
Marching men each with a bow and arrows at his waist;
Fathers and mothers, wives and children, rush to see them off;
Dust rises until the Xianyang Bridge can no longer be seen.

They cling to their clothing, stamp their feet, and block the road weeping,
The sound of their rises up into the clouds.
Those they pass along the way question the marching men;
The men simply reply, "We've been recruited so often
That some have gone to guard the River to the north at fifteen years of
      age,
And at forty are still living there in the camps, cultivating their own
      fields. . .
You have questioned us well, chief,
But do conscripts dare to express resentment?
Thus as in the winter of the year
Before the soldiers are dismissed from the Western Passes,
The prefectural officials urgently collected taxes–
Where do they expect us to provide these taxes?
We know that it is misfortune to give birth to a boy,
On the contrary it is good to have a girl.
The girl can still be married to the neighbors,
But the boy will only be buried beneath the scattered grasses."

The equally famous "Ballad of Beautiful Women" *(Liren xing* 麗人
行) of 753 seems to allude to the new chief minister, Yang Guozhong 楊
國忠, cousin of the famous imperial favorite, Lady Yang Guifei 楊貴妃:

The third day of the third month
Along the waterways in Chang'an are many beauties.
Haughty and distant, pure and upright,
Their flesh taut, their skin fine, their bodies well proportioned. . .
Warm your hands in his unrivaled powers,
But guard against approaching too near, the Chief Minister may get
angry.

But it is not only emotion that occupies the central place in a poem; Du
Fu often relies on a visit to a site or the spectacle of a landscape. This

eight-line pentasyllabic poem entitled "Writing Down My Feelings While
Traveling at Night" *(Lü ye shu huai* 旅夜書懷*)*, from 765 or 768, can serve
as an example:

> Fine grasses, slight winds on the bank,
> A tall mast, my boat, alone in the dark.
> The stars droop, the level plain seems more vast,
> As the moon gushes, the Great River sets in motion.
> How can writings bring me fame–
> I've resigned my post in illness and old age.
> Drifting and drifting, what do I resemble?
> A single sand gull between heaven and earth.

Bai Juyi 白居易 (772–846) may have enjoyed a popularity among
his contemporaries transcending that of any other poet throughout history.
During Bai's lifetime and for several centuries after his death, his glory
eclipsed that of his fellow graduate and lifetime friend Yuan Zhen 元稹
(779–831), to the point that many of Yuan's poems were attributed to
Bai. Even without these false attributions, Bai was by far the most prolific
Tang poet, leaving nearly three thousand poems in a variety of poetic
genres in addition to a large corpus of prose works. Few writers of so
long ago appear to have transmitted an œuvre so complete, one that
could provide so much material for a precise biography and that includes
so many details of a committed official career. Thus it is no wonder that
Arthur Waley's *The Life and Times of Po Chü-i [Bai Juyi]*, although written
in the 1940s, remains one of the most successful Western studies of a
Tang poet.

Bai Juyi himself took great care to ensure the preservation of his
works. They were the first literary texts in the world to be printed. Bai
paid great attention to the aural effects of his verse, to the point that
many of his works could almost be considered "oral poetry"–he enjoyed
attempting to employ the speech of the humble peasant. Duan Chengshi

段成式 (ca. 800-863), maintains that he saw a man working in the street who had had himself tattooed with the texts of Bai's poems. Bai was no less appreciated in foreign lands, especially Japan, where he remains the most popular of the classical Chinese poets. Literary critics have tended to feel uncomfortable with this precocious genius who was understood by and accessible to nearly every reader. To some extent, Bai played the role of a journalist of opinion, reporting on periods and places of crisis, and therefore he was endangered by the struggles of opposing factions, and placed at the gravest risks for supporting his friends, in particular Yuan Zhen, whose career in the government was much more successful than Bai's. Bai's satire, hidden in allegories that are sometimes obscure today, added to the reputation of a poet whose collected works also contain the most intimate and personal poems. Moreover, his two most famous poetic works are elegies. The first, "The Song of Eternal Regret" *(Changhen ge* 長恨歌), depicts the tragic love between Emperor Xuanzong (r. 712–756) and his favorite, Lady Yang. The second, "The Ballad of the Pipa" *(Pipa xing* 琵琶行), relates the emotions the poet felt on hearing an aging courtesan sing the story of her life in the capital. Now married to a wealthy merchant, her tale was told to the strumming of the *pipa,* an instrument resembling a mandolin with four strings, imported from Central Asia, that was especially favored by female popular entertainers. This second ballad of more than six hundred lines was written in 817, while Bai was serving as marshal of Jiangzhou 江州. The concluding lines read:

"Don't refuse to sit back down and play another song,
Play for me again the 'Ballad of the Pipa';"
Moved by these words of mine, she stood there a long time,
Then sat down and rapidly plucked the strings with a greater urgency.
With a chill sadness, not in her voice before,
All who sat and heard were moved to tears.
But who wept the most?
The marshal of Jiangzhou, his blue tunic soaked.

This theme has inspired a play centered on an imaginary plot in which the poet Bai Juyi, in his declining years, reveals his long-time love for this woman, about which he has remained silent for years. But the parallels in this ballad between the situation of the discarded courtesan and that of Bai Juyi–in exile when he overheard her lament–make it likely that this poem also has political overtones.

Another emotional poem (one of several on the subject) was written in 812 about the loss of his only daughter, Jinluan 金戀, literally "Golden Bell." The piece is entitled "Weeping for Little Golden Bell While I Was Ill" *(Bingzhong ku Jinluan zi* 病中哭金鑾子):

> Having a daughter is truly a burden,
> But without a son, how can one help becoming attached to her?
> It was scarcely ten days that she was ill,
> And we had already nourished her for three years. . . .
> Her old clothes still hang from the rack,
> What's left of her medicine yet at the head of the bed.
> I went with the coffin far into the village lanes,
> Saw the mound of her little grave in the fields.
> Don't say she's only a mile or so away–
> She and I are separated by eternity!

Aside from such personal verse, Bai also had a number of favorite exotic subjects that he treated in his poetry. Parrots, it would seem, were one. But was it a secret passion for parrots that Bai Juyi portrayed in the number of poems he dedicated to the bird, or did he have satiric intentions? The following poem, "The Red Parrot" *(Hong yingwu* 紅鸚鵡), written in 815, suggests the latter:

> Tribute from far-off Annam–a red parrot,
> Its colors like the peach blossoms, its speech like men's.
> So it always is for essays and arguments of us officials–
> When will we be allowed to leave our cage?

Bai Juyi offered some well-known advice about this time in the form of an eight-line poem entitled "Presented to Secretary Yang Juyuan" *(Zeng Yang Mishu Juyuan* 贈秘書楊巨源)–Yang had taught poetry to his friend Yuan Zhen. It concludes: "It is pointless to teach poetry too well, / For it's well known that it will ruin a career." This may be the case, since Bai is acknowledged as the better poet, but Yuan Zhen rose to much higher office. Bai Juyi held a complicated set of beliefs: a loyal Confucian, he encouraged Buddhist compassion, and was sometimes tempted by the alchemical aspects of Taoism. His politics were more consistent: he never stopped denouncing injustices or trying to relieve the suffering of those under his administration. Among the ten "songs" of Qin (modern Shaanxi) composed during the winter of 809, the ninth, "Dances and Songs" *(Gewu* 歌舞), ends in the following lines:

> Those guests arrives in horse-driven carriages from their mansions,
> To the storied towers of red candles, songs, and drums.
> Happily tipsy, they pull their seats closer together,
> Warmed by too much drink, they shed their fur cloaks.
> The minister of justice is the host,
> The president of the court in the seat of honor.
> Music all the day long,
> Deep in the night they cannot stop.
> Who is aware that in the prisons of Wenxiang
> Prisoners are dying from the cold?

The cold and snow of the winter of 813–specifically during the traditional calendric period known as the "Great Cold," which takes place in the final lunar month of the year, around 20 January–depicted more vividly the poverty of the peasants of his native village in a poem called "Suffering from the Cold While Living in My Home Village" *(Cunju kuhan* 村居苦寒). The image of bamboo and pine draws on the belief that these plants are noted for their ability to remain vibrant through the winter:

It's the twelfth month of 813,
For five days the snow has drifted down.
Even the bamboo and pine have all frozen to death,
How could the peasants avoid it?
As I turn and look through the village gates,
Of ten families, eight or nine are poor.
The northern winds are sharp as swords,
Their cotton clothes won't cover their bodies.
They can burn only fires of wormwood thorns,
Sorrowfully sit through the night awaiting the dawn.
As I come to realize that the Period of Great Cold has arrived,
The farmers' suffering is especially bitter.
When I think of how I pass this day,
Deep in my straw hut, the door drawn shut,
In padded clothing covered by an embroidered shawl,
Whether sitting or sleeping I have more than enough warmth.
I'm fortunate to avoid famine and frostbite,
Not to be subjected to the arduous work in the fields.
When I think of this I am deeply ashamed,
And ask myself, Who am I to escape such a fate?

A good number of his final poems are lost. But the following, written in 842, four years before his death, might serve as an epitaph–it is titled "Dazai Letian xing" 達哉樂天行 ("On Getting the Point of Taking Joy in Nature"–Letian, "Taking Joy in Nature," is also his *zi)*. The poem seems mockingly addressed to those who were hoping to inherit something from him, and it expresses the spirit in which Bai spent most of his life. The mention of "the springs of night" in the fifth line from the end may refer indirectly to the "Yellow Springs" to which Chinese souls go after death:

You've got it, got it you have, Bai Letian!
Dispatched to serve in the Eastern Capital for thirteen years!

Seventy years old before you hung up your official's cap,
Your pension not begun, you suspend your right to a government carriage.
Sometimes with fellow hikers you roam through spring's joys,
Other times with monks in the mountains you sit all night in Zen
    meditation.
For two years you've forgotten to inquire about household affairs–
The kitchen stove is seldom lit, grasses cover gate and courtyard.
This morning the cook's lad said the salt and rice are gone,
This evening the serving maids complained that their dresses were in
    tatters.
My wife and children are not pleased, my nieces and nephews depressed,
Yet I, lying filled with wine on my bed, am the picture of content.
Let me get up and sketch out my plans for you!
My schedule for disposing of my meager legacy.
First I shall sell those few acres of orchard in the Southern Ward,
Next those several hundred acres of fields by the Eastern Wall.
After that I'll sell the residence in which we live,
And obtain in all something near two million cash!
Half of this shall go to you to cover the cost of food and clothing,
Half to me to provide money for meat and wine.
This year I am already seventy-one–
My eyes dimmed, my hair white, my head dizzy.
So I am afraid I'll never use up my share of the money,
But will, like the early morning dew, return to the springs of night.
Still as I get ready to return, I certainly won't be unpleasant,
I'll dine when hungry, drink when joyful, and sleep soundly.
In both life and death there are things which just must be–
You've got it, got it you have, Bai Letian!

A display of "realistic criticism" in the spirit of Bai Juyi distinguishes
the work of eminent contemporaries such as Zhang Ji 張籍 (ca. 776–829),
Yuan Zhen, and Liu Yuxi 劉禹錫 (772–842). Du Mu 杜牧 (803–852),
although classified as one of the poets of the "late Tang," often exploits
this same vein.

3. The Late Tang. The Late Tang is the period of Chinese poetry most highly valued by a number of modern connoisseurs; the era saw the development of a kind of baroque style in contrast to the classical revivals of the Mid-Tang. This decadent age began with the brilliance of Li He 李賀 (791–817).

Although he was a protégé of Han Yu (768–824) and from an aristocratic family, Li He was unable to pursue an official career and died prematurely at age 26. His career and works have often been compared with those of John Keats. Li left only 240 poems. Charged with a strange imagery, with a bitter and morbid sensuality, a new voice in the concert of Chinese poetry can be heard in these poems, a voice only recently discovered by modern critics. There are some works, echoing *The Songs of Chu,* which are almost impenetrable to the modern reader, even with the help of commentaries. Li He preferred the relatively free form of the irregular *yuefu* verse; his "The Tomb of Little Su" *(Su Xiaoxiao mu* 蘇小小墓), written in three-word lines, about a famous courtesan of the Tang capital, may serve as an example:

Dew on secluded orchids
Like tear-filled eyes;
Where have the love tokens gone–
Here only flowers in the mist I can't bear to cut.
The grasses seems like her carriage mat,
The pine tree like the canopy.
The breeze could be her skirts,
The river her jade girdle-pendants.
In her canvas-covered carriage
She awaits the dusk;
The cold green candles
Labor to cast their shadows.
Beneath the western mound
The wind wafts the rain.

Li He visualizes here the departed courtesan reborn out of the natural surroundings of her grave–perhaps in the mist, perhaps in his mind. He suggests that he would have a love token for her, too, if he could bring himself to cut flowers from her grave-mound. As Li He stares through the mist, the poet's imagination transforms the natural scene of the tomb into one of the oil-cloth carriages courtesans used, complete with grass floor-mats and an evergreen top, awaiting the night when her soul can wander more freely. In the breeze, as soft as her skirts, and the river's rippling, he finds reminders of Su herself and confirmation of his vision. The cold green candles may be the copse of trees near the grave. Wind and rain can be merely descriptions of the weather conditions, but are also a standard euphemism for physical love between men and women. Since this figure of speech originally denoted sexual relations between a goddess and a king, and since Li He was fond of the *Songs of the South,* which depicted many surreal joinings, he may imply an eerie, surrealistic tryst here.

Scarcely less baffling is the work of Li Shangyin 李商隱 (ca. 813–858), the poet whom Mao Zedong was said to have preferred. He left nearly six hundred poems, of which the hardest to decipher are those labeled "Without Title" *(Wu ti* 無題), including the following, the second of a series of four:

> The east wind howls, as a fine mist arrives;
> Beyond the hibiscus dike, the faint sound of thunder.
> The golden toad bites the latch where the burning incense enters;
> The jade tiger pulls the silken thread, to draw water from the well.
> Lady Jia from behind peeked curtains at Clerk Han;
> Consort Fu left a pillow for the talented Prince of Wei.
> My thoughts of spring will not struggle with the flowers to blossom,
> For each inch of love in my heart becomes an inch of ashes.

In the first poem of this series, a male persona longs for a woman from whom he is separated by a great distance. Here we have the affair from the woman's point of view. The east wind and light rain are reminders to the woman of a rendezvous–wind and rain again. The second line continues to depict the natural scene (perhaps the place where the lovers first met), but also suggests that she is thinking about the man–hibiscus, *furong,* is a homophone for "his face," and thunder, possibly imagined, is often compared to the sounds of a chariot which would bring her lover home to her. Lines three and four depict the luxury of her lonely life. The incense burner shaped like a toad could be used to scent her clothing before a tryst. The next couplet contains two allusions. Lady Jia was able to catch a glimpse of the handsome Han Shou 韓壽, secretary to her father, Jia Chong 賈充 (217–282); later she had an affair with Han, which was ended when her father detected a rare scent he had given his daughter on Han's clothes. Consort Fu alludes to a woman loved by both the poet Cao Zhi and his elder brother, Cao Pi (see section II.1 above), who was also emperor of the Wei dynasty. Forced to marry the emperor, when she died she left her pillow to Cao Zhi. Cao Zhi then fulfilled his desire by meeting Consort Fu in a dream. Unlike these lovers, however, the lady of this poem, though filled with the erotic thoughts of spring, remains unfulfilled–"ash-hearted" suggests despair.

There are also a number of works in Li Shangyin's corpus which focus on non-human subjects, such as his "Elegy on a Cicada" *(Chan* 蟬):

> Always perched so high, it can satisfy itself only with difficulty,
> In vain it labors, regretting its wasted song.
> Toward dawn the cicadas break off singing one by one,
> The verdant trees remain indifferent.
> As a lowly official, my branch wavers even more,
> In my old garden, the weeds are already equally high.
> "I've troubled you, cicada, to awaken me,
> So that I and my whole family will remain pure."

In summer, cicadas fill the trees in China, droning their songs all night long. Chinese poets early on associated their song with the sadness that often afflicts the pure of heart. The poet here empathizes with the cicada, and can "understand his sound"—a euphemism for friends who truly know one another. The first line refers to the belief that the cicada maintains this purity by consuming only dew, and so it thirsts in its preferred lofty seat. Line two reveals that the cry of the cicada has failed to find it a mate—its song is thus wasted. Lines three and four suggest that as the cicada's "audience" is not moved by its song, Li Shangyin has similarly failed to impress his superiors. Lines five and six continue this line of thinking, with the poet realizing that retirement to his old home (garden) might be possible; but the final couplet reveals that he, like the cicada, will not compromise himself but will continue to sing his pure verse in the vain hope of finding an appreciative listener.

From more or less free verse to the strictly regulated poem, from the long ballad to the brief quatrain, whether popular or reserved for the initiated, Chinese poetry seems to have exhausted all the resources of the genre by the tenth century, all the themes permitted by then-current ideologies. The only possibility was to move in the direction of the popular genres. Through the medium of the courtesan's songs in the demimonde, perhaps as early as the eighth century, a new type of poem intended to be sung, the *ci* 詞 (lyric) was revealed to the scholars. By this time the new *yuefu* had essentially lost the music of its popular origins. The *ci* imposed on the composer a choice of many hundreds of melodic tonal patterns, which he had to "fill in" by finding the words, some of them from the colloquial language, which could better translate his emotions than those of the artificial, literary language.

III. The Triumph of Genres in Song

Li Bai and Bai Juyi figure among the best of those literati who chose to compose poems to be sung according to the popular *ci* 詞 (lyric) form. Wen Tingyun 溫庭筠 (812–870) was the first to achieve his literary

glory through this new genre. The first great master of *ci*, however, was
Li Yu 李煜 (937–978), the last .prince of an ephemeral dynasty that
reigned from Hangzhou over a statelet of the South during the fragmented
Five Dynasties era (907–960). Captured by the victorious Song-dynasty
armies, Li Yu spent his final years under house arrest in the Song capital,
far from his beloved Hangzhou. Li Yu's collected works consist of scarcely
more than forty lyrics, mostly evocations full of nostalgia for the splendors
of his past life spent with his courtesans, such as his "To the Tune 'A
Casket of Pearls'" *(Yihu zhu*一斛珠):

> Her evening toilet just completed,
> she adds a few light drops of sandalwood stain to her lips,
> barely revealing a clove on the end of her tongue.
> A single song in a clear voice
> for a moment breaks the line of her cherry red lips. . . .

The sadness of his captivity colors his final works, as in "To the
Tune 'The Broken Formation'" *(Pochen zi* 破陣子):

> Forty years I have passed in my country and my home–
> A thousand miles of mountains and rivers.
> Phoenix pavilions and dragon belvederes towered to the Milky Way;
> Jade trees with jasper branches created a misty dream.
> When had we knowledge of weapons of war?
>
> One morning I surrendered, a slave-like prisoner,
> I wither away, hair turned white and waist narrowing;
> The worst was to suddenly take leave of the temple of my ancestors,
> The Academy of Music played a farewell song,
> As I wept before my palace women.

Among the many other poets who gained fame through the practice
of this genre, the renowned musician Liu Yong 柳永 (987–1053) should

be mentioned. He introduced a longer form of *ci*, inspired by a popular genre called *yunyao* 雲謠 (ditties [which developed] like the clouds). His "To the Tune 'Fresh Are the Flowers of the Chrysanthemum'" *(Juhua xin* 菊花新)* may serve as example:

> About to lower the perfumed curtain and express her love,
> She first knits her moth-like eyebrows, worried that the night will prove
>> too short.
> She urges her youthful lover
> to go to bed first
> and warm the mandarin-duck quilts.
>
> A little later she abandons her uncompleted needlework,
> removes her gauze-like skirts
> to give rein to a passion unlimited.
> "Let me leave the lamp before the bed-curtains
> so that from time to time
> I may see her lovely face!"

Even Ouyang Xiu 歐陽修 (1007–1072), a serious essayist and eminent statesman, risked scandal in this genre, winning fame by not avoiding some of its more risqué themes. Witness his "To the Tune 'Night after Night'" *(Yeyequ* 夜夜曲)*:

> The floating clouds spit forth a bright moon;
> Its flowing shadows darken the jade steps.
> Although separated by a thousand miles, it shines on us both;
> How can I know what's in your heart, night after night?

The *ci* attained its full maturity with Su Shi 蘇軾 (1037–1101), better known under his literary name, Dongpo 東坡 (Eastern Slope). His *ci*, however, were only a small part of the poetic corpus of one of the greatest figures of Chinese literature–350 out of a total of nearly 3,000 poems. He based his lyrics on a style that he created, which came to be called *haofang* 豪放 (heroic and unrestricted). A sense of humor and a positive state of mind distinguish these works. His opposition to the powerful reform politician Wang Anshi 王安石 (1021–1086) earned Su Shi many exiles to the South; these exiles were difficult for the poet, but they seem to have been a source of renewal from which he drew inspiration for poems on themes such as nature, wine, and social demands. The following poem was originally "written on the yamen wall" during his first exile to Hangzhou in 1071. It lacks a formal title, but was belatedly given the following descriptive title when Su Shi returned to the city in 1090 and wrote another poem to the same rhyme: "On New Year's Eve I was on duty in the yamen, which was filled with prisoners in chains; the sun set and I was still unable to return to my quarters, so I wrote a poem on the wall." The poem reads:

> New Year's Eve, I should have gone home early,
> but I've been detained by official matters.
> I take up my brush and face them in tears–
> grieving for these prisoners in chains.
> Petty men preparing for life's necessities,
> they've fallen into the law's net without understanding their disgrace.
> As for me, I'm so in love with my meager salary
> I follow along and miss my chance to retire at ease.
> There's no need to discuss who is wise and who foolish,
> each of us has schemed so that we can eat.
> Who could set them free for a short time at New Year's?
> silently I feel shamed by those worthies of old.

The implication of the final lines is that in ancient times prisoners were freed at New Year's. Su Shi, however, who sees that he shares much in common with these men, admits that he is more worried about his job (his meager salary) than about doing what would be compassionate.

The most remarkable of Su Shi's poems are those which relate to the paintings of the literati, as he shows in the following pentasyllabic quatrain on "The Snail" *(Gua niu* 蝸牛*)*–a poem stamped with a sardonic humor, since it likely also refers to everyman's (or some particular man's) struggles:

> Its harsh slime doesn't fill the shell,
> there's just enough to moisten it.
> It climbs so high, not knowing how to get back down,
> And ends up a dried-out husk stuck to the wall.

In the following lines, composed in 1087 about a painting of flowers, Su Shi joins his conceptions of poetic art and pictorial art in his "Written on the Sprig of Flowers Painted by Secretary Wang of Yanling, #1" *(Yanling Wang Zhubu suo hua zhe zhi, di yi* 鄢陵王主簿所畫折枝，第一):

> To argue that a painting must resemble what it depicts
> Is to see it almost as a child does.
> When a poem is composed, you must go by the poem's words,
> You certainly don't need to know the poet.
> Poetry and painting basically follow the same rules–
> Heaven-given skill and originality. . . .

One of Su Shi's last poems, composed in 1100, was written to tell his dog, Black Snout that the poet had been released from final exile to the southernmost island of Hainan. The title, which also serves as a preface of sorts, reads "After I came to Dan'er I got a barking dog named Black Snout which was quite fierce but basically tame; it accompanied me when I was transferred to Hepu, and when we passed Zhengmai it swam with great strokes across the river. My fellow travelers were all startled by its actions, and thus I wrote this poem in jest:"

Black Snout, you canine of the Southern Seas,
How was I so fortunate to become your master?
By eating leftovers, you're already round as a melon,
After all, you don't have to worry about delicacies in offering.
During the day you are tame, recognizing my friends and guests,
At night ferocious, you guard the gate.
When you learned that I was to return to the North,
Wagging your tail, you were so happy you almost danced!
Leaping about, chasing the servant boys,
Your tongue hanging out, panting, raining sweat.
Unwilling to tread the long bridge,
You went straight across the clear, deep river;
Paddling and floating like a duck or goose,
Climbing on shore as rapidly as an angry tiger.
Your stealing meat was also a small fault–
So my bamboo whip had to indulge you;
You bowed repeatedly to express your gratitude;
Heaven has not given you the power of speech.
When it is time for me to send a letter home,
I know Old Yellow Ears must have been your ancestor!

The poem ends with Su Shi's tongue-in-cheek reference to Old Yellow Ears, Lu Ji's (261–303) dog who carried messages back and forth between Lu and his family.

Li Qingzhao 李清照 (1085–after 1151) is unanimously considered the greatest of Chinese poetesses, although she left us only one hundred poems, about three-fourths of them *ci*, and although she rarely treated themes other than the life of the cultivated woman in high society. Struck continually by bad luck, she expressed her emotions and her sorrows with a force previously unequaled by male or female poet. Married to Zhao Mingcheng 趙明誠 (1081–1129) in 1101, she shared her husband's tastes in art and literature. The fall in 1127 of Kaifeng, the capital of the Song dynasty, brought ruin and desolation, at a time when the couple was separated. She was inconsolable after the death of her husband in 1129; her remarriage in 1131, a painful failure. Her best poems, such as "To the Tune 'Declaration of My Intimate Feelings'" *(Su zhong qing* 訴衷情*)*, which follows, delicately evoke the joy of love for her former husband:

> Night has come, and deep in drink I'm slow to undress myself–
> plum petals stuck on a dead branch;
> Sobering up, the bouquet of wine shatters my spring sleep,
> My dream cut short, I was not able to go back.
>
> Everyone is silent,
> The moon lingers above,
> The azure blinds are drawn.
> Still I rub the remaining buds,
> Still I finger their lingering scent,
> Still I want to hold to this moment.

The poems of sadness are her most celebrated, in particular that to the tune "Each Word in Slow Tempo" *(Shengsheng man* 聲聲慢*)*, in which each character of the first three lines is repeated, creating an intensity of expression that defies translation:

> Searching and searching, again and again,
> cold and clear, clear and cold,
> it's bitter, cruel and lonely.
> That time of year when it's suddenly warm, then cold again,
> and it's hardest to breathe.
> Three cups or a couple of bowls of thin wine,
> How can they resist it–
> the violence of the wind since darkness?
> But just the passing of the wild geese
> is what struck me the hardest,
> though they are acquaintances from long ago.

Chrysanthemum blossoms pile up, covering the ground,
spoiled by a wan and sallow look–
as they are now, who could bear to pick them?
I keep vigil at the window;
alone how can I bear it getting dark?
and the wutong and at the same time a fine rain?
Until dusk bit by bit, drop by drop,
one thing follows another–
how can the single word "sorrow" convey it all?

Two images require some comment here. First, the wild geese, which long ago symbolized letters from her first husband when they were separated, have now become reminders that since his death no more letters are possible. Second, in the final stanza, the comparison between the blossoms and the poetess–both spoiled by a wan and sallow look–is certainly intended. Third, the *wutong* tree (for which there is no Western equivalent, although one translator has recently rendered it as "beech") is noted for its large leaves that produce a mournful sound in the rain.

Although concern with sound and its manipulation is evident in Li Qingzhao's works, in the hands of the literati the *ci* generally became a purely poetic form, increasingly disassociated from music. The "tunes," melodies that had been lost, became arbitrary but demanding forms, requiring a great technical virtuosity. Consequently, poets began to feel a need to renew their genre by borrowing once more from the popular sources of the song. It was in this way during the twelfth century, it seems, that the *qu* 曲 (aria) originated, a verse form that also made up the sung part of the opera-theater. The *qu* in its non-dramatic form was described as *san* 散, "occasional;" a short form, called *xiaoling* 小令, a simple strophe or refrain, was distinguished from the suites, *santao* 散套, which could be quite lengthy. Considering the difficulty of the tunes, to be sung in variable "modes," and the meaningless syllables needed to "pad" lines to fit a rhythm, the form could be written only by trained musicians, and was rarely composed by literati from the best social circles. Therefore, the themes, in which "thwarted love affairs" were often expressed, remained primarily in a popular vein. Not surprisingly, the names of the most famous dramatists were linked to these works. Thus "Springtime" *(Chun* 春, part of a series title "Songs of Great Virtue" [*Dade ge* 大德歌]) by Guan Hanqing 關漢卿 (ca. 1220–1320), who has been called by some "China's Shakespeare:"

> The cuckoo cries,
> "Go home, go home,"
> But in fact, though spring returns,
> my beloved hasn't.
> Several days of anxiousness have made me gaunt,
> As light and unstable
> as the willow fluff that flies.
> All spring there has been no word by land or sea.
> I see only
> a pair of swallows,
> their beaks filled with mud,
> building a nest.

For the Chinese the cuckoo is a poignant creature, its call seeming to echo the words "Why not go back home?" The willow fluff is a conventional image associated with the instability or ephemeral nature of a condition or situation. Here it suggests that the speaker feels adrift without her lover. The line translated as "no word by land or sea" literally refers to geese and fish, two traditional symbols for "news from someone far away," especially a loved one (see the last poem cited above by Li Qingzhao). As this woman languishes, she sees before her the bliss of a pair of swallows preparing their nest for their lovemaking.

In the long form of the aria, the freedom of language, which approaches the vernacular, allowed the absorption of some terms borrowed from the conquering Mongols (who ruled under the dynastic title of

Yuan from 1260 to 1368). This brought a lot of verve to the burlesque themes, which sometimes evoked life in the amusement quarters of the demimonde with a facetious realism.

For the last five hundred years no classical poetry has been produced that deserves to be raised to the height of its illustrious predecessors examined above. Neither the diversification of poetic production nor its amplitude was the cause of this decline. It was rather that the freshness of popular inspiration was an ideal constantly pursued and never attained.

In traditional China, poetry was everywhere. It blended well with prose in the majority of fictional and dramatic works, which were about to spread throughout various literary milieus.

Suggested Further Reading

A succinct incisive survey of Chinese poetry can be found in "Poetry," in *Indiana Companion,* I: 59–74. Entries in the *Indiana Companion* on the numerous other poets mentioned above should also be consulted. James J. Y. Liu's *The Art of Chinese Poetry* (Chicago: University of Chicago Press, 1962) and Stephen Owen's *Traditional Chinese Poetry and Poetics: Omen of the World* (Madison: University of Wisconsin Press, 1985) are fine introductions to the general subject. Burton Watson's *Chinese Lyricism: Shih Poetry from the Second to the Twelfth Century* (New York: Columbia University Press, 1971) traces the history of the *shi* genre through its major developments and is supported by excellent examples in Watson's fluent translations. The following anthologies also contain excellent translations of the major genres: Jonathan Chaves, ed. and trans., *The Columbia Book of Later Chinese Poetry* (New York: Columbia University Press, 1986); Wu-chi Liu and Irving Lo, eds., *Sunflower Splendor: Three Thousand Years of Chinese Poetry* (Garden City, N.Y.: Anchor, 1975); Victor Mair, ed. and trans., *The Columbia Anthology of Traditional Chinese Literature* (New York: Columbia University Press, 1994); Stephen Owen, ed. and trans., *An Anthology of Chinese Literature: Beginnings to 1911* (New York: W. W. Norton, 1996), and Burton Watson, ed. and trans., *The Columbia Book of Chinese Poetry: From Early Times to the Thirteenth Century* (New York: Columbia University Press, 1984).

Two Sources of Ancient Poetry

Allen, Joseph R. *In the Voice of Others: Chinese Music Bureau Poetry.* Ann Arbor: Center for Chinese Studies, University of Michigan, 1992.

Birrell, Anne, ed. and trans. *Popular Songs and Ballads of Han China.* Honolulu: University of Hawaii Press, 1988.

Hawkes, David, trans. *The Songs of the South: An Anthology of Ancient Chinese*

Poems by Qu Yuan and Other Poets. Harmondsworth: Penguin, 1985.

Levy, Dore J. *Chinese Narrative Poetry: The Late Han through T'ang Dynasties.* Durham and London: Duke University Press, 1988.

Waley, Arthur, trans. *The Nine Songs: A Study of Shamanism in Ancient China.* London: Allen and Unwin, 1955.

The Golden Age of Chinese Poetry

Chang, Kang-i Sun. *Six Dynasties Poetry.* Princeton: Princeton University Press, 1986.

Graham, Angus, trans. *Poets of the Late T'ang.* Baltimore: Penguin, 1965.

Owen, Stephen. *The End of the Chinese "Middle Ages:" Essays in Mid-T'ang Literary Culture.* Stanford: Stanford University Press, 1996.

___. *The Great Age of Chinese Poetry: The High T'ang.* New Haven: Yale University Press, 1980.

___. *The Poetry of the Early T'ang.* New Haven: Yale University Press, 1977.

Yoshikawa Kôjirô. *Introduction to Sung Poetry.* Burton Watson, trans. Cambridge: Harvard-Yenching Institute and Harvard University Press, 1967.

Yu, Pauline. *The Reading of Imagery in the Chinese Poetic Tradition.* Princeton: Princeton University Press, 1987.

The Triumph of Genres in Song

Chang, Kang-i Sun. *The Evolution of Chinese Tz'u Poetry from Late T'ang to Northern Sung.* Princeton: Princeton University Press, 1980.

"*Ch'ü*" 曲. In *Indiana Companion*, I: 220–221.

Crump, James Irving. *Songs from Xanadu: Studies in Mongol-Dynasty Song-Poetry (san-ch'ü).* Ann Arbor: Center for Chinese Studies, University of Michigan, 1983.

Landau, Julie, trans. *Beyond Spring: Tz'u Poems of the Sung Dynasty.* New York: Columbia University Press, 1994.

Lin, Shuen-fu. *The Transformation of the Chinese Lyrical Tradition: Chiang K'uei and Southern Tz'u Poetry.* Princeton: Princeton University

Press, 1978.

Liu, James J. Y. *Major Lyricists of the Northern Sung, A.D. 960–1126.* Princeton: Princeton University Press, 1974.

*"Tz'u"*詞. In *Indiana Companion,* I: 220–221.

Yu, Pauline, ed. *Voices of the Song Lyric in China.* Berkeley: University of California Press, 1993.

Chapter 4. The Literature of Entertainment: The Novel and Theater

Toward the year A.D. 1000, two major factors changed the relationship between "elite" and "popular" literature, the first intelligible to and appreciated by educated people, the second more often oral than written and aimed at for the illiterate or semi-literate. These factors were the growing divergence between the literary language and the spoken language, augmented by the increased printing of popular books, and the controversial but undeniable role of Buddhist proselytizing in seeking "access to the common people."

On the margins of the "honorable" genres–history, the essay, and poetry–emerged a printed literature of entertainment dominated by fiction. The new genre was condemned by adherents of orthodox literature. It was only in the aristocratic milieu that surrounded the conquering Mongols in the thirteenth century that these new writings were given the status of "noble literature." Near the end of the sixteenth century, some literati, among them the most prominent writers, defended the value of this new literature among themselves, but they were unsuccessful in persuading their peers. It was not until the beginning of the twentieth century, under the undeniable influence of Western literary values, that these works were seen as worthy of scholars' attention. The absence of an epic and of an ancient drama in the Chinese literary tradition deprived these new genres of the kind of scholarly validation that might have raised them to the level of poetry and prose essays. Nevertheless, their place in the literature of the people was at least equal to that of their Western counterparts.

I. Narrative Literature Written in Classical Chinese

There is a vast narrative corpus in the classical language whose themes and subjects are often considered fictional. But one hesitates to apply the adjective "fictional" to them, because their origins differ so much from the mainstream of Chinese fiction in the vernacular. Although they are referred to as *xiaoshuo* 小說, a term which in modern times is the Chinese equivalent of "fiction," the origin of this term, which translates literally as "little talks" or "minor discourses," is not suggestive of the Western concept of fiction. Xiaoshuo was able early on to extend itself to include all narrative that did not aspire to the level of the major genres. The term itself was used in *Zhuang Zi* more than two thousand years ago and now covers an immense literature which ranges from amusing stories to anecdotes, notes, or records of varied and novel events, much like the German "short story." The fact that this originally even larger corpus of materials was partially preserved can be explained, barring some fortuitous discovery in the future, by a historicist attitude on the part of scholars, who saw in these narratives sources of information, albeit not of the highest reliability, worthy of preservation. This fact, and the weakening of Confucian orthodoxy that followed the disintegration of the Han empire in the third century, emboldened some well-known scholars to "waste their time" collecting and editing such narratives.

These two factors seem to have figured in the compilation of an anthology of five hundred "volumes" of "minor discourses" published under the direction of Li Fang 李昉 (925–996), entitled *Taiping guangji* 太平廣記 (Vast Records Made during the Era of Great Peace [976–983]). Printed in 981, it became a major source for the partial reconstruction of a number of ancient short narratives.

The third and fourth centuries were the golden age for the serious scholarly recording of anecdotes. These records are of two major types: collections of bizarre events, *(zhiguai* 志怪 (records of the strange), and collections of stories about eccentric persons, *zhiren* 志人 (records of [strange] persons).

The two most famous works of the first subgenre are the *Soushen ji* 搜神記 (Records of Searching for Spirits), attributed to Gan Bao 干寶 (fl.

320), and the *Bowu zhi* 博物志 (Record of All Things), compiled by Zhang Hua 張華 (232–300). Although the original texts of most Six Dynasty collections of these narratives were lost, editors in the Ming dynasty began to reconstruct them (an effort that continues even today); the most complete extant edition of the *Soushen ji* contains nearly five-hundred brief anecdotes and tales, some of which were clearly written after the fourth century. These notes on the strange or the supernatural, which won the admiration of generations of scholars for their concision, occasionally gave way to narratives of greater length and complexity.

From the supernatural we move to the extravagant in this story of the dog from Yang, transmitted in the *Soushen houji* 搜神後記 (Sequel to Records of Searching for Spirits) and attributed to Tao Qian 陶潛 (365–427).

A young man in Yang had a dog which he liked very much and always took with him. One day, when he got drunk, he walked into the grass around a large marsh and passed out, unable to move. Winter had just arrived. A grass fire started, and the wind was very strong. The dog circled his master and barked, but the young man, being drunk, did not wake up. There was a pit filled with water up ahead, so the dog went there and got into the water. When it came back, it shook the water off its body onto the grass around the young man. It did this several times, circling its master in small steps, thereby wetting all the grass. When the fire came, the young man thus escaped being burned. He saw this only when he woke up.

Some time later, the young man fell into an empty well as he was walking in the dark. The dog howled until dawn. Someone came by. Thinking it strange that the dog was barking at the well, he went over to it and saw the young man. The young man said, "Could you let me out? I shall repay you generously." The man said, "If you give me this dog, I will let you out." "This dog has rescued me from death," the young man replied, "thus I cannot give it to you. I would gladly give you anything else." "In that case," the man said, "I will not let you out."

The dog accordingly lowered its head and cast a meaningful glance

at the well. The young man understood its meaning and then said to the
passerby, "I will give you the dog."

The man then let him out. He tied the dog and then left. Five days
later, the dog fled into the night and returned to its master.

The *Bowu zhi* lives up to its title by treating everything, especially
myths and legends–for example, this version of the story of Prince Dan
旦 of Yan 燕, the man behind a failed assassination attempt on the First
Emperor of Qin:

> Dan, the heir apparent of Yan, was a hostage in Qin. Since the
> King of Qin (the future First Emperor) did not treat him with respect
> and he could not obtain what he wanted, the heir decided to return to
> Yan and sought the permission of the King of Qin. The king refused,
> declaring absurdly, "If you can cause the crows' heads to turn white and
> horses to grow horns, you can leave." Dan looked up and sighed, and
> the crows' heads turned white. He bowed his head and lamented, and
> the horses grew horns. The King of Qin had no alternative but to send
> him back. He had a bridge built with a mechanism intended to trap
> Dan. Dan galloped over the bridge without the mechanism firing. Dan
> fled and reached the pass [where Qin's territory ended], but [it was too
> early and] the gate was not open. Dan crowed like a cock, and then all
> the cocks crowed. He thereupon returned to Yan.

The subgenre associated with memorable conduct by men and
women in their private lives is represented by the *Shishuo xinyu* 世說新語
(A New Account of Tales of the World), a collection of more than one
thousand anecdotes, compiled around 430 by the prince Liu Yiqing 劉義
慶 (403–444). This evocation of a vanishing aristocratic world has fascinated
generations of scholars seduced by the novelty of an allusive style drawing
liberally from vernacular expressions in what was then the spoken language.
A vast gallery of historical personages parades through these short
narratives, which are classified under headings that reflect a general theme

in thirty-six chapters. For example, the fourth chapter, "Letters and Scholarship," contains a number of anecdotes on these subjects. The preceding chapter presents narratives related to "Affairs of Government," and that following, those which exemplify the concept of "Squared and Correct." The following brief anecdote, the fifteenth in chapter 4, reveals clearly the witty tone of this collection.

> Yu Zisong 庾子嵩 [Yu Ai 庾敳 (262–311)] began to read the *Zhuang Zi*. When he had unrolled the first fascicle a foot or so, he put it down and said, "This is not a bit different from what I have always thought."

These anecdotes exhibit an economy of discourse reminiscent of the methods of the scholarly tradition in Chinese painting–both are the enemy of "completeness." The "emptiness" of these narratives is carefully managed by their authors, who intentionally leave spaces and things unsaid which by suggestion give life to the subject, as in the following (Chapter VII.2):

> Contemporaries depicted Li Ying 李膺 (110–169) as "brisk and bracing," like the wind beneath the sturdy pine.

What they lack is the suspense of carefully structured narratives. This step was taken with the appearance in the seventh century of "transmissions of the extraordinary" *(chuanqi* 傳奇). It is said that candidates taking the competitive examination required to obtain for official posts, which were promoted from the late seventh century on, were the first to write these tales as a stylistic exercise designed to establish their reputation and to attract the patronage of influential officials or even the examiners themselves. However, this theory cannot explain the diversity of forms and themes among the complete corpus of *chuanqi* (which ranges, according to the authority consulted, from a little over fifty tales to more than three hundred). The presence of some well-known names, such as the poet and friend of Bai Juyi, Yuan Zhen 元稹 (779–831), among the many obscure authors of *chuanqi* implies that the negative attitudes toward imaginative literature held by traditional Confucians no longer prevailed in the revitalized Confucianism of the Tang dynasty. One of the earliest scholars to take an interest in these narratives, Hu Yinglin 胡應麟 (1551–1602), felt that their fictional qualities were deliberate on the part of the authors. In other words, even when the authors seemed to be reporting actual events, their imaginations shaped and structured the narration, and their literary talents gave it a refined style. Their subtlety of observation enabled the "extraordinary" to become part of human psychology, revealing problems that were sometimes further expounded in the conclusion of the tale or in the author's comments often appended to it. The major works of this genre struck a unique balance between form and depth of emotion. The term for the genre, *chuanqi,* provided the title of a collection by Pei Xing 裴鉶 (825–880), but it became widely used to refer to these tales only during the Song dynasty.

"Gujing ji" 古鏡記 (Story of an Ancient Mirror) relates how a mirror disappeared from its case "with the roar of a dragon or the growl of a tiger on the fifteenth day of the seventh lunar month in the thirteenth year of the Daye era (617);" it is considered the earliest *chuanqi* tale and is attributed to Wang Du 王度. Not long after "Gujing ji" appeared, an anonymous tale titled "Baiyuan zhuan" 白猿傳 (The Story of the White Ape) began to circulate, satirizing the scholar and calligrapher Ouyang Xun 歐陽詢 (557–641), whose father was said to have simian features.

Shen Jiji 沈既濟 (ca. 740–800) was the author of two notable tales. The first, "Zhenzhong ji" 枕中記 (The Story of the Inside of a Pillow), takes place in 719 and exposes the vicissitudes of a long official career that turns out to have been only a dream that took the time it takes to cook a bowl of yellow millet. Li Gongzuo 李公佐 (ca. 770–848) treated a similar theme in his "Nanke Taishou zhuan" 南柯太守傳 (Biography of the Governor of the Southern Branch), linking dream tales with this formula of the futility of official life. The other tale by Shen Jiji, "Renshi zhuan" 任氏傳 (The Story of Lady Ren), is a marvellous account of the tragic destiny of this fox-courtesan whose fidelity nevertheless puts the actions of the male characters in the story to shame. The return to moral values gives a sharp edge to "Li Wa zhuan" 李娃傳 (The Story of Baby Li), by the younger brother of Bai Juyi, Bai Xingjian 白行簡 (775–826). This narrative is guided by the hand of a master–realistic details so thoroughly conceal the supernatural motifs that one searches vainly for clues that this tale was inspired by an oral account which had been elaborated through the art of a professional storyteller and based on actual events.

"Yingying zhuan" 鶯鶯傳 (The Story of Yingying), composed by the famous poet Yuan Zhen, is known to have had an immense literary impact. The "extraordinary" of this *chuanqi* is no longer the supernatural, but the femininity of the heroine, who vigorously rejects a suitor, only to join him a little later for a night of pleasure. She shows herself again only ten days thereafter, touched by a long poem which her lover decided to address to her. She returns to him each night from then on, leaving just before dawn, and invariably responding to his questions about why she does so by saying, "I am not able to act otherwise." When her lover announces his imminent departure for the capital to sit for the examinations, she easily allows him to leave, raising no objections. His repeated failures in the examinations prolong their separation and arouse her to send him letters about her burning love that the hero is proud to show to his close friends. Yet, frightened by such a passion, he decides not to return to Yingying and marry her. He justifies himself as follows:

All of Zhang's friends who became aware of this affair were astonished by his strange conduct, but Zhang's decision was firm. As I [Yuan Zhen] was on particularly good terms with him, I asked him for an explanation: "Those beautiful creatures who have been so endowed by Heaven tend to bring misfortune to others, if not to themselves. Had Miss Cui encountered riches and honor, she could have gained favor with her charm, and if she had not become clouds or rain, she would have become a kraken or a dragon: I cannot imagine all her transformations. . . . My virtue is too feeble to overcome her evil spell; for this reason I have contained my passion.

A year later Yingying becomes the wife of another, and Zhang also marries. He nevertheless attempts to see her again, but she refuses to receive him and manages to secretly send him this poem:

As I have lost weight, the radiance of my beauty has diminished,
I tossed and turned thousands of times, too weary to leave my bed.
It's not because of those in the household that I am ashamed to rise,
For you I pine away, still too ashamed to see you.

A number of other themes have been tackled by *chuanqi,* from the detective story involving a female avenger of wrongs in "Xie Xiao'e" 謝小娥 by Li Gongzuo, to the strange story of "Qiuran ke zhuan" 虯髯客傳 (The Story of the Curly-bearded Stranger) by Du Guangting 杜光庭 (850–933), which gives a part to Li Shimin 李世民, who was later to found the Tang dynasty.

In the fourteenth century, the tale in the classical language enjoyed a brilliant renaissance with the publication of a collection attributed to Qu You 瞿佑 (1341–1427), *Jiandeng xinhua* 剪燈新話 (New Tales Told While Trimming the Lamp). Among these "new tales" we find only twenty-two pieces, most of them sentimental love tales. Around 1420, Li Zhen 李禎 (1376–1452) composed a sequel, also with twenty-two pieces, titled *Jiandeng yuhua* 剪燈餘話 (Supplementary Tales Told While Trimming the Lamp). This series concluded with the eight tales in Shao Jingzhan's 邵景詹 *Mideng yinhua* 覓燈因話 (Tales Written While Searching for a Lamp), published in 1592. Dramatists and short-story writers drew on this rich material, which was appreciated by a rather large audience, who also supported many commercial editions of the *Taiping guangji*. The success that these works found in Japan and Korea saved them from obscurity, since they seem to have been considered part of the milieu that precipitated the rapid fall of the Ming dynasty in 1644 and the ideological reaction that followed, a time when many such works were censored and lost. It was not political conditions, but the futility of a genre of classical-language tales at the height of the popularity of vernacular fiction, that led to the exclusion of these works from the *Siku quanshu* 四庫全書, "complete" catalogue of the writings relative to the "four treasuries" (i.e., the classics, histories, philosophical works, and belles lettres), completed in about 1772 at the order of the Qianlong emperor.

Another factor might explain the decline of the *chuanqi:* in 1766 the first edition of the *Liaozhai zhiyi* 聊齋志異 (Records of Unusual Stories from the Leisure Studio) by Pu Songling 蒲松齡 (1640–1715) appeared. This was a collection of "strange" stories and anecdotes which had previously circulated only in manuscript. A scholar of some local note in a little village in Shandong province, Pu Songling, assuming the title "chronicler of the strange," had produced nearly five-hundred compositions based on events that came from his imagination or on conversations he had held in the course of many decades of a life in which he labored as a tutor and a secretary. Written in a refined classical Chinese, the work has enjoyed unprecedented popularity. It corrected the dryness of style of the "records of the strange" (*zhiguai*) of the third and fourth centuries with the relative prolixity of the *chuanqi.* In short, the chronicler always yields to the temptations of the story writer. We understand the fantastic of Pu Songling better than we do the realities of the time: through these voyages to the world beyond, he suggests an ironic vision of our own world.

The *Liaozhai zhiyi* inspired a number of literary emulators during the final years of the nineteenth century. *Zi bu yu* 子不語 (What the Master [Confucius] Did Not Speak Of) is a collection of irony-filled short stories in which the great poet Yuan Mei 袁枚 (1716–1798) displayed the charms of an unsophisticated style. Ji Yun 紀昀 (1724–1805) intended to oppose the *Liaozhai zhiyi* with more laconic narrations in his *Yuewei Caotang biji* 閱威草堂筆記 (Notes from the Cottage of Meticulous Reviews), gathered from collections published from 1789 to 1798. The stories of Wang Tao 王韜 (1828–1897), into which he incorporated romanticized memories of his voyages to the West, were popularly known by the flattering title "Sequel to *Liaozhai zhiyi* with Illustrations and Explanations" *(Hou Liaozhai zhiyi tushuo* 後聊齋志異圖説).

Those interested in the commercial side of letters took advantage of the opportunity to appeal to a much larger public by translating much of this literature of entertainment from classical Chinese into the vernacular. But these classical works were only one of the sources of theater and the novel. Their characteristics cannot be adequately explained without taking into account the rich panoply of oral literary genres.

II. The Theater

Although some modern Chinese critics have suggested that Chinese theater originated in the seventh century, it is impossible to trace operatic dramas, the mainstay of the Chinese tradition, back that far. These works seem to have begun in earnest in the twelfth century, especially in the burgeoning populous cities, which had amusement quarters where permanent theater halls were established. It is necessary to distinguish playbooks intended to be performed, which were of concern only to the professionals, from those which were meant to be read like novels. The playbooks were prone to reduce plot suspense in favor of lyrical outbursts. The later practice of performing only one or two acts of a drama only reinforced this tendency.

1. The Opera-Theater of the North. The origins of this type of drama are well known. Beginning in the twelfth century, a genre of "variety" entertainment known as *zaju* 雜劇 (variety plays) began to appear.

Zaju had four acts, in which one of the actors played a leading role. In the following century, it was the only dramatic form to retain a single role that was sung, following the example of recitation in a roughly contemporaneous kind of ballad called *zhugongdiao* 諸宮調–a term that has been translated as "potpourri," but approximates the chantefable of the West. In the golden age of Mongol rule (1276–1367) the *zaju* assumed its canonical form: four acts (literally *zhe* 折 or "breaks") and an optional prologue, which was rarely placed at the beginning, giving rise to its name of *xiezi* 楔子, the "inserted wedge." The astonishing flowering of the opera-theater in the thirteenth and fourteenth centuries is explained, no doubt, by the conjuncture of two factors–first, a sort of "precocious modernity," which some scholars have seen in the growth of cities, the spread of printing, the increasing mobility of the population, and the development of the coal and iron industries at this time; and second, the appreciation of operatic qualities shown by the conquering Mongols, who had little passion for formal Chinese literature (poetry and prose), but were fervent lovers of popular entertainment. There were important *zaju* dramatists throughout the Yuan dynasty and into the early Ming, including one member of the imperial family of the newly restored Chinese regime. But the preservation of this genre owes more to the renewal of scholarly interest in *zaju*, marked by the publication in 1616 of an anthology of one hundred Yuan dramas edited by Zang Mouxun 臧懋循 (d. 1621). Partly because of Zang's efforts, there are 167 extant *zaju* from the Yuan era, and 300 of the 500 produced by the Ming dynasty are still available.

Among the 108 dramatists of the Yuan whose names are known to us, a good third were from the area around the Mongol capital, Dadu 大都 (modern Beijing). That was no longer the case in the Ming; only 2 of this dynasty's 125 dramatists were from that region. The language clearly confirms the more popular nature of the Yuan pieces, despite the attempts of later editors to reduce the vulgarisms in these works. Three names stand out among the pleiad of the most famous dramatists of the Yuan:

Guan Hanqing, Ma Zhiyuan, and Wang Shifu.

The fact that little more is known of Shakespeare than about his Chinese counterpart, Guan Hanqing 關漢卿 (ca. 1240–1320), is not mere coincidence, but a measure of the low esteem in which serious scholars held all the entertainment genres. Of the sixty-odd pieces attributed to Guan, a native of Dadu, only a third are extant. In these remaining pieces, curiously, the principal role is most often entrusted to a woman. Should we grant Guan Hanqing a propensity for social satire? The most famous of his pieces, *Dou E yuan* 竇娥冤 (The Resentment of Dou E), denounces a judiciary error. A young widow is executed for a murder that was actually committed by a suitor of hers who wants to compel her to marry him.

Ma Zhiyuan 馬致遠 (ca. 1260–1325), also from Dadu, was less prolific than Guan. There are only seven known pieces by him, the most famous of which is *Han gong qiu* 漢宮秋 (Autumn in the Palace of Han). The piece is actually a retelling of a well-known story about a lady of the Han court, Wang Zhaojun 王昭君, who had to leave China to marry a northern barbarian chief. Paradoxically, it is the emperor, duped into selecting her to go, who has the principal role, which is sung. The repertoire of Ma Zhiyuan's plays reveals a predilection for Taoism, and in fact Ma belonged to one of its sects. Another of his best-known pieces, *Huang liang meng* 黃粱夢 (Yellow-Millet Dream) (translated into Western languages early in this century), was based on the tale "Zhenzhong ji" (The Story of the Inside of a Pillow) by the Tang writer Shen Jiji.

The third member of this famous trio, Wang Shifu 王實甫 (thirteenth century), was also a native of Dadu. His masterwork, *Xixiang ji* 西廂記 (The Story of the Western Pavilion), the most famous of the traditional dramas, was translated into French even earlier (1872–1880) by one of the most renowned sinologists of the nineteenth century, Stanislas Julien. This single work, which is actually a series of five *zaju*, each in four acts, is the only one left from Wang Shifu's corpus. This version of the famous

"Story of Yingying" by Yuan Zhen retains the modifications introduced by Dong Jieyuan 董解元 (fl. 1200) in his *zhugongdiao* of the same title: a happy ending and moral justification of the young woman's conduct deprives Yuan Zhen's tale of its edge while strengthening the lyricism of the story, which charmed generation after generation of young readers, men and women alike. The twenty acts of *Xixiang ji* are well below the average number of acts for the pieces in the repertoire of the Southern dramatic tradition. These plays were called *chuanqi* 傳奇, undoubtedly because they naturally drew on the sentimental themes of the artistic tales of the Tang, which were also called *chuanqi*. The longest *chuanqi* contained 130 *chu* 齣 "exits," a term that, not surprisingly, scholars have preferred to translate as "scenes." To this was added a complete disdain for the Western rule of three dramatic unities, a failure to distinguish even comedies and tragedies, and, finally, the absence of even the slightest bit of realistic scenery, symbolism taking the place of realism, so that an actor could simulate riding a horse by brandishing a riding crop as he moved about the stage. All of these factors contribute to the impression of a lack of dramatic vigor, which often troubles Western audiences and readers.

2. The Opera-Theater of the South. The *chuanqi*, which descended from the *nanxi* 南戲 (drama of the South) and originated at least as early as the *zaju* of the North, was characterized by music both sweet and languorous, costumes in more strident colors, and the predominance of sentimental themes. From the turning point in the middle of the sixteenth century, scholars participated openly in the theater and, until the eighteenth century, no longer hesitated to sign their works with transparent pseudonyms. A separate place should be accorded to *Pipa ji* 琵琶記 (Story of the Lute) by Gao Ming 高明 (ca. 1305–1370), a work in forty-two acts that exalted filial and conjugal piety. The most eminent men of letters engaged in a lively controversy at the onset of the eighteenth century, in which one side opposed the immorality of *Xixiang ji* and the other glorified the musicality of *Pipa ji*. Gao Ming's *Story of the Lute* is unquestionably the most refined of the "four great *chuanqi*" *(Sida chuanqi* 四大傳奇) of the fourteenth century, but each of the four found its own eulogist.

The musical style brought to the fore by Wei Liangfu 魏良輔 toward the middle of the sixteenth century, the *kunqu*崑曲, owes its name to its place of birth in Kunshan 崑山, near Suzhou, the economic and cultural center of the region at that time. Nearly all of the scholarly dramatists composed *kunqu,* beginning with Liang Chenyu 梁辰魚 (ca. 1510–1582).

Li Kaixian 李開先 (1502–1568) had previously introduced the rules proper to the *zaju* in his *chuanqi,* notably in his magnum opus, *Baojian ji* 寶劍記 (The Story of the Precious Sword), inspired by an episode from the saga *Water Margin* (see below).

As for the eccentric painter and poet Xu Wei 徐渭 (1521–1593), his reputation as a dramatist lies in four works of original form–*The Four Cries of the Gibbon (Sisheng yuan* 四聲猿)–considered *zaju* because of their brevity.

The eminent scholar Tang Xianzu 湯顯祖 (1550–1617) is regarded as the most well-known dramatist of the Ming dynasty, and his *Mudan ting* 牡丹亭 (The Peony Pavilion), in fifty-five scenes, is considered the most famous of his five *chuanqi.* Each of these plays masterfully exploits motifs of dreams, and they are still performed today as *kunqu,* a style that Tang Xianzu did not like at first.

The Jesuit father Matteo Ricci (1551–1610), who landed in China at the end of the sixteenth century, deplored the immoderate passion of Chinese for the theater. Officials at the highest level became involved in the theater and it would be impossible to cite all those who decked themselves so brilliantly in scandal by founding literary coteries ready to enter into the most acerbic polemics.

Shen Jing 沈璟 (1533–1610) went so far as to rewrite *The Peony*

Pavilion in order to adapt it to the Suzhou dialect (the poetic passages had to be re-rhymed, etc.). The most eminent of the Suzhou dramatists, Li Yu 李玉 (1591–1671), produced over thirty pieces, primarily satiric and didactic, most of them lost–only the titles remain to suggest their content.

The essayist Li Yu 李漁 (1611–1680)–whose name in its romanized form seems identical to that of the dramatist mentioned just above, but whose given name is written with a different Chinese character–is the author of ten *chuanqi*. Li's comedies exhibit a tone and a concern for dramatic structure unmatched in the Chinese tradition. In practice he paid little attention to the stipulations he made in his virtual treatise on dramaturgy contained in his *Xianqing ouji* 閒情偶記 (Notes Thrown Down to Pass the Time). These notes distinguish themselves from the corpus of Chinese dramatic criticism, which bogs down in inventories and rankings of dramatists and dramas or in lyric technicalities. Li Yu speaks to us as an author and director of dramas about the training of actors, having first treated the art of writing for the stage; then he concerns himself with style. The work does not slight song and music; but it is to the spoken parts of the drama that the most attention must be paid, as well as to the performance and the witticisms. A drama must be tightly knit–a necessary condition, but not in itself sufficient to sustain the interest of an audience which came to enjoy the music as well as the plot. The suspense of a carefully organized dramatic structure should be animated by a master idea and brought to life through the novelty of the theme, a liveliness of language, and the rejection of clichés. One must know how to mete out fiction and reality, how to guard against clichés and the improbable, and how not to abuse satire. It is necessary to avoid stuffing the dramatic composition with citations and allusions, or at least to avoid those which are not familiar to every member of the audience:

> Drama ought to be able to be read by the learned as well as by those who are not, by women and children. It is also necessary to prize fluency rather than depth. I have been told that for men of letters there

is no difference between composing a dramatic work and writing other types of literature; they apply themselves to show their talent; how could they achieve this easily? I would say that the ability to write a play belongs only to the greater writers.

To the tricks of the plot should be added the salt of the dialogues and the pepper of the situation, though the plot itself should flow naturally, as from a fountain; if not, it would be like

> . . . setting out in quest of pleasure by going to find a prostitute. To search for someone to sell him smiles can only result in something false : you can only draw a bitter sensuality from it.

Does a literature of entertainment merit such care? Li Yu argues that it does in his introduction:

> Confucius said, "Are there not the board games of bo and weiqi? To play them is surely better than doing nothing" (Lunyu XVII.22). Although dramatic composition can be only a minor art, isn't it still better than checkers? In my opinion, there is no major or minor art: what is important is to excel in your art. . . .

Li Yu well knew that inspiration is beyond all formula:

> To those to whom the spirit appears, the writing brush also comes. This is the measure of the man. If the brush appears, it is because the spirit has guided it there. But the man is not entirely master, because the brush conducts the spirit there or it has not wanted it at all. It is as if some supernatural creature manipulates their relationship. Can one still say of this written work that it is deliberate? Literary art is truly communication with the gods; this is not a figure of speech. The immortal works are products not of men, but of gods and demons. Man is only their plaything.

Li Yu took the Chinese theater in a new direction. After him the *chuanqi* produced two masterpieces before dying out, yielding its place to troupes of professional players who performed according to playbooks written by anonymous authors, playbooks that were rarely printed. This final period of dramatic development, which saw the birth of what is called in English "Peking/Beijing Opera" *(jing xi* 京戲, literally "drama of the capital"), belongs more to the history of entertainment than to the history of literature.

Hong Sheng's 洪昇 (1645–1704) *Changsheng dian* 長生殿 (The Palace of Eternal Youth), completed in 1688) dealt with the popular but tragic love story of Emperor Xuanzong (r. 712–755) of the Tang and his favorite, Yang Guifei. In a pattern that was repeated often at the beginning of the Manchu dynasty, Hong Sheng had his characters, who were ostensibly living in the Tang dynasty, comment on events that were clearly more related to the late Ming dynasty, and the play was therefore judged "indecent" (read "seditious) by the Kangxi emperor (r. 1662–1722) himself; the official career of the author was ruined, on the technicality that Hong had presented the premiere during a period of mourning for a member of the imperial family.[4] Despite the ban, the piece was acclaimed for its lyricism.

Even when simplified, the plot of *Taohua shan* 桃花扇 (Peach–blossom Fan), with its forty scenes (not counting the prologue and epilogue), is too complex to be laid out here. By Kong Shangren 孔尚任 (1648–1718), it is the most representative work of the trend toward a preference for quasi-contemporary themes in the novel and drama at the time of the fall of the Ming dynasty. The events surrounding the collapse of the Ming

---

[4]Another, more recent example of a conflict between politics and drama can be seen in the PRC government's refusal to allow a new production of *The Peony Pavilion* to be performed or travel abroad because it was "feudal, superstitious, and pornographic" (see the series of articles on this in *The New York Times,* 25 June–1 July 1998).

furnished the context and the framework for the play. The author, a descendant of Confucius in the seventy-fourth generation, had been working on this piece for nearly fifteen years when it was first performed in 1699. From its portrayal of the hated dictatorship of the eunuch Wei Zhongxian 魏忠賢 (1568–1627), which lasted from 1620 to 1627, to its depiction of the rivalries that tore apart the refugee court of the Ming dynasty in South China several decades later, the work was a powerful evocation of the imperiousness of the defeated, who, despite their failure, did not lack men of valor. The Kangxi emperor, who asked Kong for a preliminary reading of the play, found it only of lukewarm interest: without proscribing the piece, he decided to dismiss the author from his services, since Kong Shangren had made too clear his attachment to the defunct Ming regime. The title of the play is an allusion to the fan that Hou Fangyu 侯方域 (1618–1655), then a young militant scholar, offered to the beauty Li Xiangjun 李香君. Forced to join the house of a corrupt high official as a concubine, Li attempted to commit suicide by bashing her head in; her blood splattered onto the fan, and one of her artistically gifted friends transformed these bloodstains into peach-blossom petals.

In the *chuanqi*, in contrast to the *zaju*, all of the roles are likely to participate in the singing. The chantefable thus seems to be the common origin of both these great dramatic genres, which still entertain audiences, albeit select audiences, even today.

III. The Novel

There is not a work of Chinese novelistic literature in the vernacular that does not preserve some of the conventions of the professional storyteller. The modern reader of the novel, of course, pays little attention to these devices, such as direct address to the reader. The clear bond with oral literature would seem to merit further research into this relationship, a direction for research that has recently been found to be fruitful. This work has dispelled the accepted notion that the conquering Mongols brought the two new genres of drama and the novel to the Chinese from outside China.

The use of the vernacular in the theater, a necessity because classical Chinese is not intelligible to the ear, led to the spoken language becoming "literary" after a time. In the novel, the bond between proto-forms of the novel and orality justified its use.

1. Oral Literature. Oral literature was not simply the "threepenny opera," inexpensive entertainment that even the lowest class of peasant could afford. It existed long before this kind of entertainment. Moreover, Chinese oral literature catered to the elite as well. If we can perceive in oral literature an antiquity and a diversity, it is only in that part of it which has been passed on by writing and even printing. Written texts in the colloquial language may have been meant to be read aloud to the illiterate. Yet the proportion of totally illiterate people in China was probably much lower than in the West. They formed, nevertheless, a crushing majority of China's people, in particular of its women. Besides those who were illiterate, there remained a large semi-literate population, even though China enjoyed a common language and writing system. Writing was a method of transmission of oral literature and allowed amateurs and professional performers, often only marginally literate, to restore these texts to their proper function, which was to be heard.

A major archaeological discovery at the end of the last century, which was made entirely by chance, yielded the history of more than a thousand years of oral literature. More than one–hundred texts known as *bianwen* 變文 were discovered among some thirty–thousand fascicles taken from a grotto-library which had been sealed by monks in 1035. This discovery in grottos known as the "Thousand Buddhas" near the northwestern city of Dunhuang essentially restructured the field of early "oral" Chinese literature. The majority of these texts are chantefables, but there are also examples written entirely in verse or prose. The language used ranges from a vulgarized classical Chinese to something approaching the spoken language. The themes are sometime profane, and for the most part are common to the subjects of numerous other popular literary forms. It has been shown that the term *bianwen*, long interpreted as "texts changed" or "transformed" (into vernacular Chinese), actually means "texts on the scenes [of the life of Buddha] in pictures." The *bian* were "rolled," *zhuan* 卷, in a way that allowed them to be shown as the story was told. One of the most characteristic and best-articulated texts is a long version of the story of Maudgalyâyana (Mulian 目連 in Chinese), whose impious mother fell into the depths of the final and most terrible of hells. Instead of passing into *nirvâna,* the pious disciple of Buddha, left to search for his mother and extracted her deliverance from the Great Sympathetic One.

Following the example of Theodor Benfey (1809–1881) and subsequent scholars, it was tempting to take up again, mutatis mutandis, the thesis that these marvelous stories had their origin in India. China's intelligentsia–which in the early part of this century was made up largely of occidentophiles, a situation that resulted from the continuous adulation of all things Western during the "May Fourth Movement" (4 May 1919 until about 1942)–enthusiastically supported the idea that the corpus of imaginative literature in the colloquial languages had foreign origins, an idea they believed improved the image of these genres. Near the end of the 1950s, however, the Chinese regime of Mao Zedong, denounced the error of this position of national denigration. The question remains controversial; it has received only qualified responses to date.

Over the course of the one-thousand-year history of Chinese oral literature, most of its genres have disappeared, giving way to new forms that developed under new names. Each genre was able to find its audience, some in the numerous popular milieus of town and countryside, some in more affluent circles, even those of the imperial court. Certain genres have been able to inspire admirers, and learned imitators have left texts for us. It is significant that the professional storytellers, originally called *shuohuaren* 説話人, "tellers of stories," became in the seventeenth century *shuoshude* 説書的, "tellers of books." Telling tales had by then become an art that people worked at full-time. The techniques used were not merely spoken; there were also genres that displayed the talents of singers and musicians. These talents were sometimes combined in a performance by a single person; at other times the performance group would include two or even (less commonly) three people. As a general rule, storytellers worked from memory, but they might be helped by a synopsis, by a text from another literary genre which served as the primary material, or by notes on prepared passages and formulaic expressions. As soon as a text by an author of a certain genre–a text that might never have been performed–approached something like a novel, it was characterized as a narration in the popular language composed for a silent reader. Such seems to have been the case for some *tanci* 彈詞 (ballads [accompanied by stringed instruments] strummed), a genre completely in verse, composed and performed by women for a female audience. But *tanci* were also intended to be read, as with *Zaisheng yuan* 再生緣 (Ties for the Next Life), the masterpiece by Chen Duansheng 陳端生 (1751-ca. 1796) consisting of more than 500,000 words, or with *Tianyu hua* 天雨花 (Flowers Falling in the Rain), composed in thirty volumes by Tao Zhenhuai 陶貞懷 during the nineteenth century.

In short, though the novel reached higher levels among the public, it still touched the lower strata. These oral genres, on the other hand, which lacked vocal and musical support when they were read silently, often found themselves reduced to fictional narratives that approached the novel. This "neutralization" through writing led to other distinctions within the novel based on the dimensions and thematics of the work.

2. Stories and Novellas. The birth of the novel in the vernacular seems tied to the origins of the inexpensive "popular" book. The invention of printing responded to this demand, as well as to the needs of the

Buddhist proselytizers. The extremely rare surviving examples of ancient woodblock printing are primitive in appearance, mostly short fascicles revealing a clumsy technique. The thesis that has long prevailed would have us believe that some of these small booklets were produced as prompts called *huaben* 話本 (base of the narration or story), for the storytellers, which were then imitated by writers for the reading audience. In fact, certain texts, among the most ancient extant, seem to be clumsy attempts to reproduce a session by a teller of *xiaoshuo*.

From various types of ancient evidence, we know that specializations in storytelling had developed by the twelfth century. "Little talks" (*xiaoshuo*) were the least prestigious, but the most popular. Their strong point was to be able to offer the public a complete narrative in one session and a varied range of themes. Perhaps the tellers took turns according to their specialties, with those who specialized in romantic subjects narrating to the accompaniment of a flute.

In the amusement quarters, where such short stories were produced, bookstores published the texts of stories or ballads, as well as the scripts of successful dramatic works, in thin, "disposable" booklets. None of the originals have come down to us, but a few of them may appear in re-edited form in the *San yan* 三言 (Three Words), an anthology of 120 stories published by Feng Menglong 馮夢龍 (1574–1646) from 1620 to 1625. Some of the stories gathered early in this century by Miao Quansun 繆荃孫 (1844–1919) in a collection that is probably apocryphal may have originated as such texts; the publication of these stories in 1915, under the title *Jingben tongsu xiaoshuo* 京本通俗小説 (Short Stories Which Could Be Understood by Common People in the Capital Edition), caused a sensation, by bringing the nobility of a venerable ancestor to the trend toward using the spoken language in literary works.

The *Jingben tongsu xiaoshuo* contains texts of astonishing maturity with respect to the art of storytelling and the handling of the spoken language. An introduction to the principal narrative, usually an anecdote or a series of poems, left the audience time to settle into their seats and created suspense that was skillfully maintained by the tempo of the narration. Although claiming provenance in the Song dynasty, the work seems much later.

The most ancient extant collection of *huaben,* dates to the Ming dynasty. Titled *Liushi jia xiaoshuo* 六十家小説 (Stories of Sixty Tellers), it brings together sixty *xiaoshuo* and seems to mark the first scholarly interest in the genre of "popular" short stories. It was compiled from 1541 to 1551 by Hong Pian 洪楩, a descendant of Hong Mai 洪邁 (1123–1282), the editor of the *Yijian zhi* 夷堅志, the largest collection of anecdotes ever gathered. Hong Pian published a series of six volumes, containing ten stories each. Only twenty-nine pieces remain, two of them in fragments. Eleven more were recovered from later collections. These are narratives that stem from different oral genres; none are divided into chapters or sections. Jacques Dars has recently provided a complete French translation (Paris: Gallimard, 1987) under the alternate title *Contes de la Montagne sereine (Qingping Shantang huaben* 清平山堂話本) referring to the name that Hong Pian gave his publishing house, "Hall of Mount Qingping" (Qingping Shan Tang 清平山堂), perhaps alluding to a place in the environs of Hangzhou.

From 1620 to 1625, Feng Menglong published an anthology of three volumes containing 120 *xiaoshuo* in Suzhou and Nanjing. With four stories in each, the three volumes purported to have an edifying aim and were known collectively as the *Three "Yan"* 三言, or "three words," because each of the titles ended in *yan.* Feng's publication ensured the *huaben* a popularity that lasted only until the end of the seventeenth century. Feng was left the task of sometimes repairing original texts and sometimes concealing his creation of new stories–thus he referred to the works in the collection as both "ancient and modern."

Ling Mengchu 凌濛初 (1580–1644) profited from Feng's commercial success, and published, in 1628 and 1633, two other volumes of the same dimensions as the *San yan*. Unlike Feng, however, he openly portrayed himself as their creator. The title of these two volumes, *Pai'an jingqi* 拍案 驚奇 (Striking the Table in Amazement at the Wonders), also dismisses the pretense of edification in favor of a new concept of the "extraordinary" in daily life. From the two hundred total stories in these five collections by Feng and Ling, forty were chosen for the anonymous anthology *Jingu qiguan* 今古奇觀 (Wonders of the Present and Past), which appeared in about 1640 and attempted to take advantage of the popular taste of the day. Portions of this collection have frequently been translated into various Western languages. It was the great and lasting popular success of these forty stories that hastened the sources of the collection into an oblivion from which they emerged only in the twentieth century. The forty works chosen for inclusion may be debated, but *Jingu qiguan* includes some stories that are incontestably "modern" masterpieces. "The Courtesan's Casket" (more precisely "Du Shiniang nu chen baibao xiang" 杜十娘怒 沉百寶箱 [Du the Tenth in Anger Sinks the Casket with One Hundred Treasures]) develops a powerful drama that recalls one of the themes of *The Idiot* by Dostoevsky, when Nastasia throws a large packet of bank notes (the price offered for her hand by a suitor) into the fire. The courtesan Du, flouted and betrayed, throws herself into the waves after the casket. She has hidden its existence and its treasures from her lover, a young scholar from a good family. He hopes to kill two birds with one stone by jilting her: to escape from the displeasure of his father and to earn one-thousand taels of silver by giving her up to a rich salt merchant. This tragic denouement, exceptional in the Chinese narrative tradition, seems characteristic of the period of transition from oral storytelling to literati imitations of these tales. The ending occurs suddenly, at the end of a long description of the psychological behavior of the partners. The lover can decide to reveal his "excellent plan" to Du only after having passed a part of the night sighing in her arms. Is she taken in by her lover's despair, which is really only a cover for his bad conscience? She is not duped, but feigns agreement, before throwing into the waves, drawer by drawer, the treasures of her casket, thereby denouncing the lechery of the salt merchant and the venality of the young scholar; finally, she follows her treasures into the waters.

The first story of Ling Mengchu's *Pai'an jingqi* opposes this moral and psychological "extraordinariness" to a "relativized extraordinariness" on the theme of luck that turns. A son goes into business to help his family avoid financial ruin. Bad luck pursues him in each of his ventures, however. He finally decides to go abroad and forget about his failures for a while, taking with him only a crate of a local variety of tangerines, known as "red delicious of Dongting Lake," to quench his thirst. At one port, where each person is left to attend to his own affairs, the young man remains on board the boat:

> He was sitting in melancholy; suddenly the oranges returned to his mind: "This crate of oranges, which I have not opened since we left, has probably become spoiled in the heavy atmosphere of my cabin. . . . Let me take advantage of the others' absence to have a look at them!" [He decided to spread them out on the deck.] The entire boat became a brilliant red; from afar one would say there were a thousand lights, a sky filled with stars. . . . Passersby on land approached and formed a crowd. . . . (The most curious were bold and offered a piece of silver). . . . Hardly had he opened it when a delicious perfume titillated their nostrils and drove those pressed around him to exclamations of surprise. The buyer, who had watched Wen eat his orange, peeled it as he had. But, not knowing any more about how to eat them, he stuffed the whole thing into his mouth rather than separating it into quarters. His throat filled with juice; he swallowed it without spitting out the seeds. "Marvelous, marvelous!" he exclaimed with a huge sigh. *(Pai'an jingqi,* I/1; *Jingu qiguan,* 9)

As a result of his trip, Wen earns a fortune selling the tangerines and goes on to become a successful exporter.

The majority of such "modern stories" were free expansions on sources in the classical language. That was no longer the case in many later collections, which did not enjoy such sustained popularity. One sometimes suspects another type of source: various facts and scandals which were the object of "handwritten stories," possibly distributed in the form of printed sheets of paper. At the time of the fall of the Ming, the short story became more overtly involved in the politics and conflicts of the times. West Lake in Hangzhou offered a geographic framework for many of these works. The technique of the *Decameron* of Boccaccio, with the plot of each story relating to the main theme of the collection, so common in Indian literature, was used in only a single known Chinese collection, the *Doupeng xianhua* 豆棚閒話 (Idle Talk under the Bean Arbor), an anonymous work.

The essayist Li Yu (1611–1680) also wrote innovative works of this type, employing them in defense of his right to be inventive in constructing plots related to a central theme. Their artifice is revealed in the skillful use of irony, through which the creator makes fun of himself and his creation, and in the clarity of a style in which Li fully masters the resources of the spoken language. Published between 1654 and 1658, Li's first collection of stories bore the significant title *Wusheng xi* 無聲戲 (Silent Dramas), which fell unjustly into oblivion in the eighteenth century. Several of these twelve pieces, followed later by sequels, furnished subjects for his dramas. They were eclipsed by the lasting success of his *Shi'er lou* 十二樓 (Twelve Towers), novellas each developed over several chapters.

The *Rou putuan* 肉蒲團 (Prayer Mat of Flesh), the masterpiece of the erotic novel, exhibit the qualities and manner typically associated with the Chinese novelist. We will not attempt to recount the plot, as clever as it is extravagant, apart from emphasizing the Buddhist framework that gives the narrative the allure of a sort of Tantric initiation. This work shows the hand of a connoisseur in matters of lovemaking, not the work of a simple drudge. In chapter 6 the hero discusses his "projects" with his mentor and sworn brother, Rival of Kunlun–that is to say, rival of the protagonist of the Tang tale "Kunlun nu" 崑崙奴 (The Slave from Mount Kunlun), written by Pei Xing (825–880). The Kunlun slave, endowed with extraordinary powers, abducts for his master a beautiful woman with whom the latter has fallen in love. But the go-between for the hero in *Rou putuan* is scarcely a measure of the hero's ambitions:

> "Big brother, don't worry about that too much. The other day I bought an excellent aphrodisiac, which I have here. Right now the only problem is that I have no woman. That leaves a hero without a place to display his arms. If only a 'happy event' can be arranged, before undertaking the job I will do a little rubbing and smearing; then I will not be afraid that it won't last long."
>
> Rival of Kunlun replied, "The aphrodisiac can only make this thing last longer, but it cannot make it bigger. If those whose 'capital' is big and thick use the aphrodisiac, they will be like those talented candidates who took ginseng tonic before taking the official examination. After they enter the examination hall, they will surely be full of energy and able to write good compositions. As for those whose 'capital' is tiny, they are just like those who have passed the qualifying examinations but have nothing in their bellies. Even if they had taken tons of ginseng, they still could not do a good job upon entering the examination hall. . . ."

In twenty chapters, *Rou putuan* is a typical example of the kind of "short novel" that appeared at the end of the sixteenth century; this also became the favorite length of the sentimental novel, referred to as fiction in the *caizi jiaren* 才子佳人 "men of talent and beautiful women" mode. In vogue from the middle of the seventeenth century until the middle of the following century, its conventional situations, embellished by polygamous "happy endings," titillated Western taste. Novels in this subgenre were accordingly among the first Chinese literary works to be translated.

The version of *Haoqiu zhuan* 好逑傳 (The Fortunate Union) published by Thomas Percy in 1761 showed the Western public how much the mysterious Chinese were like the Europeans in their sentimentality. John Francis Davis offered a less distorted translation of the novel in 1829. This eighteen-chapter work succeeded in China because of entertaining characters such as Tie Zhongyu 鐵中玉 (Jade within Iron), despite the Confucian "puritanism," not typical of the *caizi jiaren*narratives, surrounding the courtships in this tale. Haoqiu zhuan inspired the unfinished novel *Kyôkaku den* 俠客傳 (Stories of Heroism) by the prolific Japanese novelist Takizawa Bakin 滝川馬琴 (1767–1848).

Yu Jiao Li 玉嬌李 (ca. 1660) is considered the model of sentimental fiction. The title of this anonymous work, like that of *Jin Ping Mei* 金瓶梅, is formed from the names of the three heroines. Arcade Huang, Montesquieu's informant on matters of the East, began a translation that Abel Rémusat finished in 1826 and that Stanislas Julien revised and published under the title *Deux cousines* (Two Cousins) in 1842. In 1860 Julien published a careful version of another sentimental novel, *Ping Shan Leng Yan* 平山冷燕 (here again each of these syllables is taken from the name of a character in the novel), under the title *Les deux jeunes filles lettrés* (Two Young Women of Letters).

However, it was not in these works, said to be of "medium length," that Chinese readers of the novel were able to satisfy their passion–a passion so widespread that the eminent scholar Qian Daxin 錢大昕 (1728–1804) denounced *xiaoshuo*, claiming that it was as destructive as the heterodox sects of Buddhism and Taoism. This passion could be satisfied only in those lengthy works of fiction, often of composite authorship, known as "long novels" or sagas.

3. The "Long Novel" or Saga. More than a hundred chapters, a million or more characters–such is the finalized form to which traditional editions of the long novel aspired at its peak. The long novel could pride itself on having put onto the market the "four great extraordinary books," *sida qishu* 四大奇書, in the first quarter of the seventeenth century, each chapter of which was illustrated by two full-page woodblock prints. Next to these long novels, the Confucian "Four Books" cut a poor figure. These four masterpieces of the long novel at the end of the Ming dynasty also represent the major subgenres of the form: the historical novel, as seen in the *Sanguo zhi yanyi* 三國志演義 (The Three Kingdoms); the swashbuckling novel, typified by *Shuihu zhuan* 水滸傳 (Water Margin); the fantastic novel, as defined by *Xiyou ji* 西遊記 (Journey to the West); and, finally, the novel of behavior and morals, such as *Jin Ping Mei* 金瓶梅.

The origin of the long novel seems to hark back to the most honored category of professional storytellers–the historical narrative related in cycles told over long periods of time. The distinction was maintained throughout the long history of this art, so that oral narrators of the "major books," *dashu* 大書, which celebrated the important historical affairs of China's past, were opposed to those of the "minor books," *xiao shu* 小書, which related the domestic events of daily life. Because the oral historical narratives were never accompanied by songs or musical instruments, they were called *ping [hua]* 平話, "plain [narratives]," although some scholars prefer the term "narratives with commentary" or "commenting narratives." *Pinghua* designates an oral genre that is still alive today, but it has also served for many centuries as a synonym for the novel. Japanese libraries have preserved five printed texts from the fourteenth century, each a separate popularized version of a history of a different Chinese era, re-edited from originals of the preceding century. In these texts, characterized as "completely illustrated plain narratives" *(quanxian pinghua* 全相平話), there are illustrations at the top of each page. The *Sanguo zhi pinghua* 三國志平話 (Plain Narrative on the Records of the Three Kingdoms) is only three chapters long, but some of its passages are more popularized than the corresponding sections of the long novel *The Three*

Kingdoms. This novel, in 120 chapters, was attributed to one Luo Guanzhong 羅貫中, who some have argued should be identified with a fourteenth-century dramatist by the same name. The large number of novels attributed to this obscure figure, however, raises suspicion. We do not have any evidence of an edition prior to 1494 of the longer version–i.e., the novel–titled *The Three Kingdoms.* This text, moreover, is not thought to derive directly from the *pinghua* account of the same period. Nothing enables us to confirm the hypothesis that the *cihua* 詞話 (narratives interspersed with poems to be sung) is an intermediate stage between the *pinghua* and the long novel. The fact remains that *pinghua* reveal a scholarly concern for the greatest conformity with the "official" historical sources, themselves often considerably "folklorized." The *pinghua* were then presented in a more civilized style approaching that of classical Chinese. Thus, for example, in the *pinghua* on *The Three Kingdoms* period, one cannot find the legendary account (as it appears in the prologue to the novel) claiming that the parties who struggled for hegemony in the tripartite division of third-century China were headed by reincarnations of the companions who helped found the dynasty (in 206 B.C.) and who were unjustly executed at the instigation of Empress Lü 呂 (r. 195–188 B.C.).

In short, the amplification–*yanyi* 演義 (development of the sense)–of the novel *The Three Kingdoms,* although reputed to be "seven-tenths fiction," offers an example of the historical novel much different from our own: history is not the framework, but the subject of the fiction; the latter insinuates itself into the text only to give more color and life to the narratives, a popularized chronicle of the past.

The "first" of the four great long novels–there is a known edition of 1522–*The Three Kingdoms* was the last to receive its definitive form in the hands of Mao Zonggang 毛宗崗 shortly after 1660. This restructured version of the novel with new commentaries superseded all previous editions and remains much more popular than the edition prepared by Li Yu (1611–1680), who strove to be more faithful to earlier versions. It is impossible to summarize here the struggles and intrigues of this novel as the three powers search to reunify China, each for its own profit.

Innumerable works of opera-theater and other genres of entertainment have drawn on material from *The Three Kingdoms*. Cunning occupies a place as important as warfare in this colorful novel, the most popular Chinese work in other East Asian cultures. The character who exemplifies cunning is Zhuge Liang 諸葛亮, the wise counselor of Liu Bei 劉備: Zhuge's disappearance foretells the ruin of his master. A proverb puts the reader on guard: "In youth, do not read any of *Water Margin;* in old age, stay away from *The Three Kingdoms.*"

The action of *Water Margin* is set in the thirteenth century: not one of the great novels takes place in a contemporary setting. Nevertheless, no one considers *Water Margin* to be a historical novel, because the story does not belong to "history" as such. Its subject matter, rebellion, was often eschewed in official writings. Various extrapolations lead us to conclude that the nucleus of the novel took its form from what were called *xinhua* 新話, "new narratives," used by storytellers to present recent events. It is generally accepted that *Water Margin* was compiled in the fourteenth century and directed against the Mongols who then controlled China. We have been unable to confirm this. On the contrary, since the end of the fourteenth century, eccentric scholars have read it as a denunciation of the Chinese imperial government's abuse of power. The novel is structured around a chain of events and permits almost any interpretation: versions of *Water Margin* range from 71 to 124 chapters, and the debate over precedence between the fuller-text versions and the simpler-text versions remains unresolved. Paradoxically, the simpler texts generally include a greater number of episodes. But the strength of the novel is in the ability of its author to strike a style appropriate to the theme of rebellion: never before had the vigor and resources of the spoken language been handled with such mastery.

Was *Water Margin* an expression of the presumed author's indignation against the incompetence of the constituted powers, as Li Zhi 李贄 (1527–1602), the accursed philosopher, would assure us, or was it an exercise in literary style, as Jin Shengtan 金聖嘆 (1610–1661) attempted to demonstrate in his admirable commentaries? The fascination exerted by the novel fit precisely with its resistance to any too-coherent interpretation. The band of outlaws that swelled through the course of the narrative was not made up of choir boys. The pleasure of reading the novel is precisely its length, a feeling no excerpt can convey. It does not matter if only about 40 of its 108 heroes are memorable: what is important is the long-range view of the swirling world of the novel. Various episodes or "mini-cycles" have inspired dramas and works in many other popular genres. Considered an incitement to banditry, in 1642 *Water Margin* was the first of the great novels to be officially banned. The band of outlaws ends the novel by joining with the imperial regime to combat other rebels. Jin Shengtan, arguing that the novel should be appreciated primarily as a literary monument, eliminated a good third of the final part in such a way that the epilogue became a dream predicting the imminent massacre of the outlaws; critics have condemned the commander-in-chief of the rebels, Song Jiang 宋江, even though he rallied his comrades to the ideals of "fidelity and justice." The *Shuihu zhuan* in 70 chapters (or 71 and a prologue) has eliminated rival editions for nearly three centuries. Inspired Marxist critics in the People's Republic attempted to make the work an epic of peasant revolt, although in the strictest sense peasants are distinguished by their absence among the outlaws of *Shuihu zhuan*. At the turning point of the Great Proletarian Cultural Revolution in 1972, the novel emerged from the global negation of classical literature to be denounced for its "revisionist" theme and to have its "traitorous" main character, Song Jiang, opposed to the impulsive Li Kui 李逵, the Black Whirlwind and the "true revolutionary" in the work.

The first great novel to have been re-edited in this last phase of the Cultural Revolution was the *Xiyou ji*, an apparent paradox, since the theme of the extravagant *Journey to the West* was the quest for salvation through the Buddhist faith. Inspired Marxist critics read this story of an ape endowed with supernatural powers who led a troupe of pilgrims west out of China in search of Buddhist scriptures and concluded that the "Promethean side" of the main character, Monkey, should be interpreted as the reincarnation of the revolutionary spirit of the Chinese people. In the past a number of scholarly commentaries have sought to systematize the allegory in this novel, especially within a Taoist framework. In fact, this work is like the other three great classical novels: it is possible to assume a coherent allegory only in a novel written by a single author ex nihilo, but these sagas were the creations of a "composite authorship" and evolved over a long period of time. This resistance to systemization by critics is undoubtedly the secret of the long-term popularity enjoyed by these vast novelistic creations, works that readers immersed themselves in without ever being sure that they had grasped the key to the story. It would be somewhat tedious to continue the joke over one hundred chapters, but the laugh brings salvation; besides, the extravaganzas are related with unmatched gusto. Nevertheless, a conscious mastery in structuring the whole underlies an apparently reckless story.

Here also the point of departure is historical: the pilgrimage of the monk Xuanzang 玄奘 (602–664) in quest of the Buddhist scriptures, the most famous of a number of such trips. Departing the Tang capital of Chang'an in 629 without authorization, he was received with the highest imperial honors upon his return in 645. Xuanzang was able to get an important team appointed to translate the Sanskrit texts that he had brought back–nearly a third of the entire Chinese Buddhist canon, an undertaking without parallel from the point of view of both quality and quantity. In *Journey to the West,* Monkey, the hero of this enterprise, is only the protégé of the four monsters or animal spirits who have become Buddhist converts, converts arrayed against the covetousness of the demons along the way who seek to devour a piece of flesh from this completely abstinent holy monk, since one mouthful would make them immortal. Of these four animal spirits, the horse-dragon speaks in only a single episode, and Sandy remains most often a secondary partner. The emphasis is on Pigsy and Monkey, the first being a kind of Sancho Panza to the second. But there is no doubt that Monkey attracts all of the footlights. The first seven chapters are devoted entirely to him, from his birth out of a rock "impregnated" by Heaven, to his capture and confinement under a mountain. The central role was already allotted to Monkey in an earlier printed version of the story dating to the twelfth or thirteenth century, which may in turn derive from a ninth-century text, a *shihua* 詩話, narrative interspersed with poems, composed in the style of Buddhist *gâthâ* poetry. Could it be because the monkey is the animal associated with the west in East Asia? Or because it symbolizes the unrest of the human spirit? The most complete edition of *Journey to the West,* dating to the end of the sixteenth century, is also the earliest version of the story in the novel format; it insists on the latter interpretation without managing to sustain the allegory of "monkey = troubled human spirit" from beginning to end. Critics still face an insoluble textual problem concerning the priority of a "full" version of the novel and an "abridged" one. The literary superiority of the first over the other versions, however, is uncontested; the reliability of the attribution of *Journey to the West* to Wu Cheng'en 吳承恩 (ca. 1500–1582) remains unconfirmed. Was it a work which did not take itself seriously but was received as a serious work, or just the opposite? Should one enjoy the humor in it or bring out its irony? This ambiguity makes the novel a unique work, without parallel in world literature. An example of the humor so characteristic of the narrative comes from chapter 98, when just before meeting the Buddha, the monk Tripitika sees his mortal remains floating in the river, Monkey having pushed them into a boat without a bottom:

> The patriarch gently punted the small boat away from the shore, when they turned to find a corpse floating down the stream. Seeing that the venerable monk was terrified by this view, Monkey laughed and said, "Master, do not be afraid at all! In fact, that is you!" "It is you, it's you," Pigsy joined in chorus. In his turn Sandy then applauded: "It's you, you!"
>
> The boatman uttered a cry and also exclaimed, "But that's you! Congratulations, congratulations!"
>
> All three joined in a single voice to offer their congratulations.

In the penultimate chapter, Guanyin, while glancing through the reports of the protective deities, notices that the number of terrible trials that the Chinese monk must undergo is not complete.

> In Buddhism, nine times nine is necessary to find the truth. Since the holy monk has suffered eighty tests, he still lacks one. We did not know he had spared himself of completing the number.

The object of the quest–seeking Buddhist texts–seemed derisory in relationship to the merits accumulated through the eighty-one tests and to the brilliant arrival at their goal, the Western paradise. . . .

At first examination, nothing could be more different from *Journey to the West* than the *Jin Ping Mei* 金瓶梅 (Plum Flower in a Vase of Gold), other than that they share the same number of chapters, one-hundred. In fact, some other similarities could be pointed out, such as the limited number of principal characters in both novels or the use of the cycle of the seasons as a chronological reference in the narrative. We know, through the correspondence of a coterie of scholars, including some of the most prominent of the time, that the originality of the novel dazzled the few privileged persons who had access to the incomplete manuscripts at the tail end of the sixteenth century. Many Chinese critics of the May Fourth Era (1919–1942) vaunted the modernity they found in this novel.

Drawn from an episode narrated in chapters 23-27 of *Water Margin,* the *Jin Ping Mei* in effect is of the dimensions of a saga or long novel. As a result, in spite of various developments in subplots and digressions, the main plot, with a number of hidden links, resembles that of the shorter novel. The "realism" of *Jin Ping Mei* does not lie simply in the "little details that are true;" it translates the passion of the teller of "minor stories" or *xiaoshuo* into the tiny details that organized daily life, suspends the action, and brings out the feelings of things and people. The wealth of erotic descriptions is elevated more by curiosity than by indulgence. These descriptions have caused the first great novel of Chinese morals to be forbidden, inaccessible to the public at large, although it has been recognized throughout Chinese literary history as a masterpiece. The career of the huckster who is the protagonist of this work, Ximen Qing 西門慶, a collector of women, reaches its apogee exactly at the middle of the novel. If the last quarter of the narrative carries on without him, it is because the true center of interest is that emphasized by the title, which contains the names of two of his concubines and a temperamental maidservant.

The edition refined and commented upon by Zhang Zhupo 張竹坡 near the end of the seventeenth century is a long-unrecognized masterpiece of literary criticism; the concept of alternating "hot and cold" is developed remarkably by the commentator, who, following the example of his predecessor, Jin Shengtan, denounces the treachery of Song Jiang and condemns the principal wife of the Ximen Qing, Golden Lotus 金蓮, as abusive, reprehensible, and weak.

In the 1930s, an old printed edition dating to 1618 was discovered. Labeled a *cihua* (narrative interspersed with verse to be sung), a primitive stage of the novel, the text has no prologue, but rather employs a brief "oblique" tale on a related theme to open the narrative in the age-old style of the storyteller. These clues weaken the generally accepted thesis that this work was the first creation of a single author (albeit an unknown author) in the realm of the novel. The vigor of the editing and the structure seems to preclude the notion of one personality who might have imposed on this work a vision of the world close to that of Xun Zi, the Confucian philosopher of antiquity who felt that human nature was fundamentally bad; did human nature not find in the corrupt society of that time, conveniently re-situated in the thirteenth century, that with which to satisfy its worst tendencies? Yet a careful examination of the text reveals that the author presumed to leave a manuscript that was incomplete. His breathtaking erudition touches the domain of entertainment literature, particularly that in the vernacular, from which he has selected and skillfully employed a good thousand fixed expressions. One finds in the novel a marquetry of texts cleverly joined and adapted to the needs of the narration. Quarrels and problems occupy a large place in the text, along with the "schemes" of the master of the house to crush the weakest of those who oppose his designs. Inspired Marxist critics take pleasure in using, or abusing, the qualifier "naturalist" to condemn this work, which otherwise embarrasses them by honoring no taboos, as we can see in the following excerpt from chapter 72, depicting Ximen Qing in bed with one of his concubines just after they have made love:

> Ximen Qing felt the need to get down from the bed to urinate. But the young woman refused to let go of [the penis which she had kept in her mouth].
> "My dear," she said to him, "piss in me, if that is troubling you. I will swallow it all! It's good to stay warm, you should avoid the cold. It would be better than getting down and freezing your balls off."
> "My dear little cookie, no one loves me like you do!" Ximen Qing exclaimed, immensely happy with such attention.
> At this he pissed to his heart's content into her mouth. She actually drank it, slowly, mouthful after mouthful, without losing a drop.
> "Is it good?" Ximen asked her?

"A little bitter. If you have some jasmine tea, it would help to make that taste go away. . . ."

Dear readers, let me tell you that such is in general the conduct of a concubine, who will resort to anything to bewitch her husband. She will have no shame before the most humiliating indulgences. Never would a legitimate wife, who prides herself on her eminent position, stoop to such practices.

The reputation that has resulted from such passages should not cause us to forget the other facets of the novel, an incomparable source of information on society at the end of the Ming. The work marks a turning point in novelistic technique in the coherence of its vision and the meticulousness of its descriptions. It explains the appearance in the following century of works that became indisputable modes of individual expression. Chief among such works is the *Honglou meng* 紅樓夢 (Dream of the Red Chamber), a search for a lost time which was no more than a dream of the splendors of a life spent among girls in the women's quarters of an aristocratic Manchu residence.

The work was published for the first time in 1791–1792 in 120 chapters. But it had circulated since 1754 in a half-dozen unfinished manuscripts presenting numerous variants, none of which went beyond chapter 80. The authenticity of the 40 final chapters remains a subject of controversy. The wealth and variety of the commentaries have not ceased to feed critical studies of sprawling proportions. The identification of the author, Cao Xueqin 曹雪芹 (1715–1763), is in the end the only point on which there is unanimity, rightly or wrongly. Was the novel a sort of "sentimental education" or, as Mao Zedong, who boasted of having read it five times, would have it, an "encyclopedia of Chinese feudal society in its decline?" One could hardly put it better than the major commentator, a relative of the author, who claimed in a marginal note that the novel was inspired by the *Jin Ping Mei*, but explored the sentimental rather than the erotic side of love. The novel shows the same predilection for the closed world of what seems to be a heavenly garden. The allegorical and marvelous framework brings a coloring more Buddhist than Taoist to the work, playing on the reality and fiction underlying the sufferings that threaten when the enjoyment of life in the enchanted world of childhood and adolescence comes to an end. It goes without saying that this seems a radically original novel to the Western reader: the development of feelings of love in a doomed and unauthentic world, a position in a sense diametrically opposed to that of the *Jin Ping Mei*, where sensual passion destroys. It is also the outcome of an intellectual current descended from the preceding centuries. The prologue explains this:

> After having heard this sort of discussion [on the originality of this work, which completely differed from the little sentimental or erotic novels], the Taoist monk Vanitas was lost in thought. He reread carefully the Story of the Stone. . . noting that in it one spoke only in general of the sentiments of love, and that it held to a faithful relationship with facts, without even attempting to reproach or harming morals and inciting to debauchery. . . . From this time on the Taoist monk Vanitas realized that from emptiness sensuality emerged, from sensuality love was born, through love one entered sensuality, and from sensuality one awoke to [the true meaning of] emptiness [that all nature is illusory]; in consequence he changed his name from Vanitas to Amor and modified the title of the *Story of the Stone* to *A Record of the Amorous Monk*. Kong Meixi, from the homeland of Confucius, suggested calling it *Precious Mirror for Lovers in the Breeze and Clarity of the Moon*. Later, Cao Xueqin, having worked on it for ten years in his study "Nostalgia for the Red," reworking the text five times and establishing a table of contents and a chapter division for it, titled it *The Twelve Beauties of Nanjing* and added an introductory quatrain:
>
> > Pages filled with words insane,
> > Handfuls of harsh, bitter tears.
> > All say the author is crazy,
> > But who can understand its true flavor?

The alternate title *Story of the Stone (Shitou ji* 石頭記) is explained by the fact that the hero of the novel, Jia Baoyu 賈寶玉, was born with a piece of jade in his mouth, which was his life itself; Baoyu means "precious jade," and his family name "unauthentic." Baoyu spends his last years among the young women of the residence, girls whose purity is that of "clear water," as he puts it, whereas he, like other young men, is "fashioned of mud." He is insanely in love with his sensible and sickly cousin Lin Daiyu 林黛玉, who dies in despair when Baoyu is compelled to marry another cousin, the wise and saintly Xue Baochai 薛寶釵. A number of other subplots are linked to this general line of the narrative, peopling the novel with memorable characters who are depicted in pure spoken language, reputed to be close to Pekingese, with an unaffected style of incomparable poetic power.

This maturity in the art of the novel, set, however, in a language closer to that of the vernacular of Nanjing, can be found in an unfinished work left by Wu Jingzi 吳敬梓 (1701–1754), *Rulin waishi* 儒林外史 (An Indiscreet Chronicle of the Mandarins [better known under the title *The Scholars]).* The earliest extant edition of this satiric masterpiece dates to 1803. Its fifty-five chapters constitute an episodic structure that exercised a decisive influence on this subgenre at the end of the nineteenth and the start of the twentieth centuries. Although *The Scholars* has a sarcastic tone completely different from that of the *Dream of the Red Chamber,* the two works share the characteristic of being a mode of individualized expression for literati to leave reality in a way that previously had been seen only in literary criticism. The principal theme of the novel is a devastating criticism of the "system of examinations," the key to the vault of the imperial regime and to the bureaucratic Chinese society we commonly refer to as "feudal."

[In chapter three the wretched scholar Fan Jin has finally received the "baccalaureate," which qualifies him to participate in the highest examinations to qualify for an official position; however, he must pay

the costs of the trip to the provincial capital. His father-in-law, Butcher
Hu, whom he has asked for financial help, retorts sharply:]

"Don't waste your time! You think of yourself already as a 'gentleman,'
although you are only a leprous toad dreaming of eating the flesh of a
wild swan. I have heard it said that your success was based not on your
compositions, but on your advanced age–the chief examiner accorded
you the title out of pity. Now, poor fool, you imagine yourself 'His
Lordship!' All those who achieve such status are stars in the literary
constellation in heaven. Haven't you remarked that the 'lords' of the
Zhang family in the village possess a fortune worth millions, and that
each is endowed with a square face and large ears [suitable for high
rank]? With your beak-like mouth and ape's chin, you would do better
to piss on the ground and view your reflection in that pool!." . . But Fan
Jin became, contrary to all expectations, "His Lordship,"
and–literally–deliriously happy: the shock of the announcement of his
success rendered him unconscious. His father-in-law at first dared not
lay a hand on this eminent person, but, after much prompting, decided
to give him a "congratulatory slap."

The nineteenth century witnessed the birth of other subgenres of the
novel. Among the most curious of these is that labeled "the scholarly." It
is represented by the masterpiece by Li Ruzhen 李汝珍 (ca. 1763–1830),
Jinghua yuan 鏡花緣 (The Destiny of the Flowers in the Mirror), a novel
of a fantastic journey, subtly structured, and known especially for an
episode in which the hero lands in a country where the positions and
duties of men and women are reversed.

The most lively popular successes were reserved for novels of the
so–called "Wuxia" 武俠 (chivalric or martial-arts) school and for those of
the judiciary-case school (a kind of detective novel featuring well-known
judges from history), both containing fantastic adventures. The proliferation
of the novel testifies to its increasing numbers, but it must be added that
none of these products could aspire to the standards reached by the

masterpieces of the seventeenth and eighteenth centuries. The reading of novels, an activity primarily of women, children, and young men, was more than ever considered unworthy of a mature scholar during the nineteenth century. The literary influence of the West was necessary before the vernacular novel could be rehabilitated among the literati.

Thus it was in classical Chinese that Lin Shu 林紓 (1852–1924) brought nearly two hundred works of fiction to the notice of the public, having first published his version of *La Dame aux camélias* in 1899. Meanwhile, the abolition of the traditional examination system in 1905 sounded the death knell for this language of the scholars. The diffusion of the old-fashioned entertainment genres facilitated the triumph of the spoken language, referred to as "modern Chinese," in literature beginning about 1920. But the modern novel, modeled on its Western counterpart, although written in the language of the people, long remained confined to educated circles. Does this mean that classical literature will henceforth be a thing of the past? No one would dare affirm that the crisis of cultural identity in China would be reduced by shelving classical literature. At the very least, one could claim that the quality of modern or contemporary production has not eclipsed that of the past.

The recent renewal of interest in traditional literature, the "search for roots," shows that the rupture between the modern and traditional literatures is much less complete than it appeared, that the bonds which unite the two are even more solid and more numerous than those which connect the literatures of the West to their Greek, Latin, and other ancestors.

Suggested Further Reading

The essays on "Drama," "Fiction," and "Popular Literature" in the *Indiana Companion* (I: 13–30, 31–48, and 75–92, respectively) provide ready access to more information on the subjects of this chapter. Individual entries on the numerous other novelists, story writers, and dramatists, their genres, and their works can also be found in the *Indiana Companion*.

Narrative Literature Written in Classical Chinese

Dudbridge, Glen. *The Tale of Li Wa*. London: Ithaca Press for Oxford University, 1983.

Kao, Karl, ed. *Classical Chinese Tales of the Supernatural and the Fantastic: Selections from the Third to the Tenth Century.* Bloomington: Indiana University Press, 1986.

The Theater

Birch, Cyril. *Scenes for Mandarins: The Elite Theater of the Ming.* New York: Columbia University Press, 1995.

Chang, Hsin-chang. *Chinese Literature: Popular Fiction and Drama.* Edinburgh: Edinburgh University Press, 1973.

Crump, James I. *Chinese Theater in the Days of Kublai Khan.* Ann Arbor: Center for Chinese Studies, University of Michigan, 1990.

Dolby, William. *A History of Chinese Drama.* London: Paul Elek, 1976.

Idema, Wilt, and Stephen West. *Chinese Theater from 1100–1450: A Source Book.* Wiesbaden: Harrassowitz, 1982.

Johnson, David, ed. *Ritual Opera, Operatic Ritual: "Mulien Rescues His Mother" in Chinese Popular Culture.* Berkeley: Institute of East Asian Studies, 1989.

Mackerras, Colin, ed. *Chinese Drama: A Historical Survey.* Peking: New World Press, 1990.

Shih, Chung-wen. *The Golden Age of Chinese Drama.* Princeton: Princeton University Press, 1976.

The Novel

Dudbridge, Glen. *The Legend of Miao-shan.* London: Ithaca Press for Oxford University, 1978.

Hanan, Patrick., trans. *The Carnal Prayer Mat.* Honolulu: University of Hawaii Press, 1996.

___. *The Chinese Short Story: Studies in Dating, Authorship and Composition.* Cambridge: Harvard University Press, 1973.

___. *The Chinese Vernacular Story.* Cambridge: Harvard University Press, 1981.

Hawkes, David, trans. *The Story of the Stone.* 5 vols. Harmondsworth: Penguin, 1973–1986.

Hegel, Robert E. *The Novel in Seventeenth-Century China.* New York: Columbia University Press, 1981.

Hsia, C. T. *The Classic Chinese Novel: A Critical Introduction.* New York: Columbia University Press, 1968.

Idema, Wilt L. *Chinese Vernacular Fiction: The Formative Period.* Leiden: E. J. Brill, 1974.

King, Gail Oman. *The Story of Hua Guan Suo.* Tempe: Center for Asian Studies, Arizona State University, 1989.

Ma, Y. W., and Joseph S. M. Lau, eds. *Traditional Chinese Stories: Themes and Variations.* New York: Columbia University Press, 1978.

Mair, Victor H. *Tun-huang Popular Narratives.* Cambridge: Cambridge University Press, 1983.

Plaks, Andrew H. *The Four Masterworks of the Ming Novel: Ssu ta ch'i-shu.* Princeton: Princeton University Press, 1987.

Roberts, Moss, trans. *Three Kingdoms: A Historical Novel, Attributed to Luo*

Guanzhong. Berkeley: University of California Press, 1992.

Rolston, David. *Traditional Chinese Fiction and Fiction Commentary.* Stanford: Stanford University Press, 1997.

Shapiro, Sidney, trans. *Outlaws of the Marsh.* 2 vols. Bloomington: Indiana University Press, 1981.

Sung, Marina. *The Narrative Art of Tsai-sheng yuan.* San Francisco: Chinese Materials Center, 1994.

"Wu-hsia hsiao-shuo." In *Indiana Companion,* II: 188–192.

Yang, Hsien–yi, and Gladys Yang, trans. *The Scholars.* Peking: Foreign Languages Press, 1973.

Yu, Anthony C., trans. *Journey to the West.* 4 vols. Chicago: University of Chicago Press, 1976–1983.

___. *Rereading the Stone: Desire and the Making of Fiction in a Dream of the Red Chamber.* Princeton: Princeton University Press, 1997.

INDEX

M

N

S